Let Your Light Shine

If you are a Christian, here's news for you: you are being watched. Christians are trying to stand straight in a world where everyone else is bent and twisted from the crippling effects of sin. Christians are obvious. The very gospel they believe makes them an instant target. The very light they embrace for their salvation emanates from them, revealing the miserable condition of those around them.

In words like these, *Glow in the Dark* illuminates Paul's letter to the Philippians. This devotional guide will explore themes such as living for Christ, having His attitude, meeting the needs of others, and the place of suffering in Christian experience.

Six daily readings each week for twelve weeks.

Glow
in the
Dark

Glow in the Dark

Rick Bundschuh

Illustrated
by
Rick Bundschuh

Regal Books

A Division of GL Publications
Ventura, California, U.S.A.

To Tom Finley and Ira McDuck
One for pushing
One for pulling
Both for carrying

Rights for publishing this book in other languages are contracted by Gospel Literature International (GLINT) foundation. GLINT also provides technical help for the adaptation, translation, and publishing of Bible study resources and books in scores of languages worldwide. For further information, contact GLINT, Post Office Box 6688, Ventura, California 93006, U.S.A., or the publisher.

Published by Regal Books
A Division of GL Publications
Ventura, California 93006
Printed in U.S.A.
Library of Congress Cataloging in Publication Data applied for.

CONTENTS

Week   1   Grow in Character   9

Week   2   To Live Is Christ   21

Week   3   Suffering Is Part of the Bargain   31

Week   4   The Needs of Others   43

Week   5   The Attitude of Christ   55

Week   6   Glow in the Dark   67

Week   7   Lost and Found   79

Week   8   Hitting the Goal   91

Week   9   No Other Gods   103

Week 10   Rejoice   115

Week 11   Dwell on These Things   125

Week 12   Be Content   137

Week One

GROW IN CHARACTER

Day 1 No Shallow People

> *And this is my prayer: that your love may abound*
> *more and more in knowledge and depth of insight,*
> *so that you may be able to discern what is best and*
> *may be pure and blameless until the day of Christ,*
> *filled with the fruit of righteousness that comes*
> *through Jesus Christ—to the glory and praise of*
> *God.* Philippians 1:9-11

It is an odd and tragic fact that through our various contacts with other people most of us have run into those who could have their entire lives, personalities, and thought-lives summed up and explained in a matter of minutes. They are the poor souls who have put everything that they are and think into one barrel and then fired it, point-blank, at those they come in contact with. In other words, they are people with very little true meaning and content in their lives. All that you see about them is all that there is.

They are the shallow people. They have no depth of character, no dimension, no mystery, and no intrigue.

Shallow people often make a positive first impression—a huge initial entry. They may impress us with their intensity, they stun us with their beauty, they amaze us with their energy. They have to, for there is nothing else behind that initial impression that can be offered. They are bankrupt of real quality.

It is not that shallow people do not have the capacity for depth, it is that they have never chosen (or never learned) to develop or dig out the wells of beauty in their lives.

Starting shallow is no crime. Most of us started swimming lessons in water where we could easily touch bottom. While we were young, the shallow end of the pool was quite satisfactory and safe. But the lure of the deep end eventually overwhelmed us and we finally ended up enjoying depths that a few years before we had no interest in. The flaw is not in the shallowness but being content to stay there.

Our culture (as shallow as it often is) has even recognized

the most blatant of these puddle swimmers. We give them disparaging names like "bubble brain" or "airhead" and have even cast them countless times into the role of a "dumb blonde." In doing so, most in our culture can go to bed at night assured that they are not among the shallow people, while they invest the total of their lives in pursuit of sex, wealth, popularity, thrills, chills, power, or some other plaything of the wading pool set. Get past the facade of the "Don Juan," "trend-setter," or "fashion plate" and there is a hollowness. The energy of life has been misspent and ill-invested.

Being shallow does not prevent us from becoming Christians. In fact, most of us come to the realization of our own shallowness at precisely the time we recognize our need for God. We recognize that there is a deep end to life that we are compelled to experience. It is impossible to remain shallow and still be transformed into the kind of creatures that God wants us to be. God means to impress His image upon us; this gives us our depth and dimension. He takes flat, petty people and carves into them ridges and valleys of His love. Those who resist the Master's molding remain in the twilight of the Christian experience. It takes no depth to enter the "narrow gate," but a few steps further along in the Christian journey rests a sign that says "NO SHALLOW PEOPLE."

Please note that depth is not dependent on intellectual capacity but upon the willingness to love and learn from Christ. It is possible for the village idiot to have a deeper understanding of the important things of life than the college professor has.

The world may lay many charges at the feet of Christians. Shallowness should never be one of them.

What could you do that would increase your depth and wisdom as a Christian?

Day 2 A Way That SEEMS Right

*I give you sound learning, so do not forsake my
teaching.* Proverbs 14:2

Hiking along the switch-backed trails of the High Sierras is
a tough and sometimes monotonous journey. The boredom
of the terraced trail is usually broken by stopping to look at the
sheer beauty of the wooded tapestry that spreads below and
the barren peaks hurling themselves up in front of you.

Occasionally, and especially when it is growing late or
when one is getting impatient to reach the destination, there
seem to spring up shortcuts—alternate routes that could take
considerable distance off the switchbacks in exchange for a
small bit of extra effort.

Most often these detours take the shape of a narrow goat
trail that winds vertically above the trail connecting with the
next level of the path.

For many hikers there are times when those little shortcuts look so attractive that they decide to change course. "It
seems best to take this way," they reason. It seems quicker
and adventurous, but it is ultimately foolish.

The first thing that most who wander off the trail in search
of the "easy way" discover is that the vertical angle of the goat
trail is more than anticipated. The weight of the gear on their
back acts as a magnet pulling them backward. They often
finds themselves groveling up the hillside rather than climb-
ing. The next thing common with a goat trail is that the composition of the shortcut is considerably more crumbly than
the well-packed trail. Rocks, both large and small, dislodge
just as you put your trust in them. Smaller gravel underfoot
gives way until you find that you are in a dance of one step forward, three slides back. Plumes of dust chase each rock down
the cliff and then blow back up again, coating the climber in a
pale swath of filth.

At some point in the climb up most "shortcuts" it
becomes apparent that what seemed the best route was not
only the hardest but didn't place the thrill-seeker any further

ahead. In fact, the adventurer must often gives up his "trail" and retraces his steps or try to catch up to his partners who have long since passed him by following the traveled trail.

Knowing the best way to live should be a characteristic of all who take the name Christian. But it is not always so. God's way does not always seem fun; our way may seem quicker and more satisfying. His way seems routine, our way seems adventurous. But ultimately His way is better and wiser. We can choose and discern what is the best only if we follow the way marked out for us by the guide of all life. Anything less will only result in defeat, wasted energy, and a battered and torn soul.

Describe any shortcuts you have been tempted to take rather than to obey God. What do you think people should do if they find themselves on the wrong trail?

Day 3 To Know What Is Real

> *Yet when I surveyed all that my hands had done and what I had toiled to achieve, everything was meaningless, a chasing after the wind; nothing was gained under the sun.* Ecclesiastes 2:11

James "Waldo" McAllister was one of the chief clowns in the youth group. He was always quick to crack a joke or participate in some stunt (usually at the expense of someone else). If there was anyone who deserved a taste of his own medicine, it was Waldo. I guess that is why I can still remember so clearly when good ol' Waldo got his just deserts. The youth group had set up camp at an eerie but fascinating spot in the high desert called "Ghost Town." It was, in fact, the remains of a once prosperous gold mining venture that had gone bust almost a century before. There was little of value left standing in what had once been a bustling town. Except for a number of abandoned mine shafts dotting the hills, the place might easily have been mistaken for the decaying rubble of a half-dozen deserted homesteaders' claims.

The site had been chosen not only because of its history but also because of the fine sand dunes nearby and great motocross terrain.

Kids who had never before made the trek almost predictably asked the same questions when they spotted the remains of the old mines on the hills. "Do you think there is any gold left around here?" Usually the answer was no, but this year the youth pastor and a couple of accomplices had prepared a surprise. Each pocket was full of "fool's gold" (in reality, it was molten lead dropped in water to create a nugget shape and then spray-painted gold). "Ya never know," replied the clowning clergy, "maybe some rich, lost vein got washed up during this year's rain."

Meanwhile, the coconspirators were busy unloading the nuggets around the campsite. It was not too long before a sucker took the bait. Waldo came charging up to one of the staff secretively clutching the "lead gold" to his chest. "Is it gold?" he whispered hopefully.

"Well it sure looks like gold, and it weighs about what you'd think gold would weigh," came the reply, straight-faced.

For the next few hours Waldo went berserk. He came rushing up with fistfuls of treasure begging for a ballpark appraisal. "Wow! Could be $50 or $60,000 worth by now, Waldo." By the end of the ploy Waldo had not only made his fortune but, at least in his mind, had spent it as well.

When it came time to let Waldo in on the joke he simply wouldn't believe it. Even when the nuggets had been broken in half exposing the dull grey lead Waldo still insisted that he was a rich kid. Eventually, the truth crept up on him and his empire built with lead came crumbling down. It took him the rest of the day to find any humor or forgiveness for the good-natured con-job that he had bought into.

Unfortunately, there are a good number of "Waldos" running around the world today, madly grasping what they think is of value only to be surprised that they are left holding a fistful of lead scattered for them by the adversary who is doing anything but joking around.

Perhaps that is one reason why it so important to understand and know what is of real value in life and what is treasure for fools.

Make a list of foolish things in which people invest their lives.

Day 4 The Strange Case of the Carbonated Cockroach

Do not be hasty in the laying on of hands, and do not share in the sins of others. Keep yourself pure.
1 Timothy 5:22

Before aluminum cans took over as the chief container for all soft drinks, most beverages were contained in returnable glass bottles. This was both a blessing and a curse. It was a blessing because the roads were not littered with discarded cans and unreturnable bottles, and because an enterprising little kid could scrounge quite a bit of pocket change by bumming the empties off friends, family, or neighbors.

The curse was that the bottles collected in every conceivable corner of the house and attracted ants, spiders, and cockroaches with their sticky residue. Many people were not organized enough to remember to take the empties to the store with them every trip, so their garages often turned into a giant storehouse of bottles. Once the bottles were taken to the store they had to be handled by the store management, money had to exchange hands, and most frustrating of all, bottles were rejected because the store didn't happen to carry that brand of beverage.

The bottles were then transferred to a central bottling plant where they were cleaned and refilled. This may sound like no major job but considering the condition of some of the bottles that I remember returning, it would have taken a super cleaning job to make them fit for human use again.

The bottling company had special machines that peered through the empty bottles to make sure they were clean after the initial super-scrub in the super bottle scrubbing machine. These machines were quite marvelous and not only completely cleaned and sterilized each bottle but checked for nicks and cracks that would make them unfit for sale. Bottles that didn't come clean or were cracked were tossed.

For the most part, this system worked well. I trusted it completely—until one hot summer day.

Four of us were sitting on the curb outside Willy's Hobby Shop. Old man Willy had every kind of plane or rocket motor imaginable, as well as fantastic models and radical war stories that he would tell all of the kids who hung out around his store. But even more special was the soda machine that worked overtime and actually froze half of the beverage. The result was more of a slush than a soda.

As we were swigging our drinks, suddenly the friend next to me gasped, sputtered, and spit. "Ugh! There's something in this drink!" he coughed. He stood to his feet as he said it and by the toe of his tennis shoe we saw the sadly drowned remains of a very carbonated cockroach. Our friend went crazy and flung the bottle into the street and went running around spitting for the next half hour. The rest of us laughed like mad and then carefully examined our bottles in the glistening sunlight—just to make sure. In fact, from that day on, having lost complete trust in the efficiency of the bottling machines, I checked every bottle I bought for little surprises before I drank.

Most of us would respond with disgust to any impurity in what we physically consume. It would pay us well to be as cautious and disgusted with impure things that we are tempted to digest in our minds and hearts.

Make a list identifying some things to watch for that would be impure input into your life.

Day 5 Love and Knowledge

> *If I have the gift of prophecy and can fathom all*
> *mysteries and all knowledge, and if I have a faith*
> *that can move mountains, but have not love, I am*
> *nothing.* 1 Corinthians 13:2

Knowledge can be very dangerous. It is much like the muscles in the body—very nice to have when you need to lift some heavy obstacle in your way, but not so great when someone is looking around for help in carrying the waterbed upstairs—still full.

Knowledge at an unbelievably escalating rate is available at the mere touch of a computer keyboard. One graph shows the increase in available knowledge (that is, the known of all things that are to be known) going at a small gradual scale—maybe a bar or two per century on typical graph paper, until the twentieth century. At that point, the graph shoots straight up off the graph paper and goes for five miles! This kind of knowledge can lead one to the dangerous conclusion that the simple availability of data will help one to live a better or more successful life.

Of course, many of the problems that mankind has muddled into have not come from the lack of knowledge but rather from the blatant disregard of the knowledge that is already known. For instance, it is probable that Christians of our century have more actual Bible knowledge than did the large majority of early Christians (many of whom were illiterate). But it seems from history that they did a great deal more with the knowledge that they had than we have done with our great bounty of biblical information.

By itself, knowledge is cold and sterile. Alone, knowledge can deceive one with a false sense of pride. Perhaps that is why in many passages where knowledge is mentioned it is wedded to some other benevolent partner. Love gives knowledge the vehicle to express itself. For example, one may have the knowledge of certain medical skills but use them only to line the inside of a purse or wallet. The skill may have some value but the possessor is stripped of all the worth that could have been his if he had used knowledge with genuine love.

Love can also work the other way around as it dances with knowledge. You may have so much love for people that you seek the knowledge of a skill (such as medicine) with the motive of helping people.

It is this kind of insightful love that uses knowledge to its fullest. Knowledge apart from it chokes on its own self-indulgence.

How important do you think education is to God. Why?

Day 6 The Best Is What Really Matters

> *Blessed are they whose ways are blameless, who walk according to the law of the Lord. Blessed are they who keep his statutes and seek him with all their heart. They do nothing wrong; they walk in his ways.* Psalm 119:1-3

"You get what you pay for," the salesman said with the flat tone of voice that not too subtly suggested, "You'll be sorry."

"This receiver looks just like the top-of-the-line model and it costs half as much," replied the slightly perturbed customer. "Besides, with the money I save on this set I can afford to buy a gob of new albums."

Obviously fighting submission to the old motto, "the customer is always right," the salesman gently commented, "Well, sir, I hope that you are satisfied with your purchase. But keep in mind that it is what you can't see inside this stereo that makes the price difference."

The customer smiled and thought to himself, "Always trying to squeeze out the extra buck; this will be the last time I shop here!" Several hours later he was at home with his new receiver and a stack of new albums scattered over the floor.

Within a month one of the channels in the stereo began to cut out, followed soon after by the pungent smell of smoke streaming through the receiver's vents. The set sparked in agony and died a violent death. The irate customer stormed back to the store only to find out that the company which had produced the set had gone belly up and would not honor his warranty. He spent the difference between the low-and-high-price sets in repair costs.

Most of us (except for the most frugal) want the best. We select our clothes, instruments, cars, and fast food based on what we think is best. If nothing else, we at least recognize what is best even if we can't afford it. If the item is really important, we strive to get the best possible. Ironically, in the one area where the best is the most important, many are more than satisfied with good or fair.

This area of neglect is in the spiritual realm—in the choices and ideas that we live by. Many see the best, but the price is just too high to pay.

Often, the best is not easily come by while things of secondary quality can fulfill the need for instant gratification, which seems to be the driving force behind many in our society. God's way is always the best, though not always the easiest, the quickest, or the least painful. But then, in the end, you get what you pay for.

Create a list contrasting things that are God's best with similar things which are not as good as His plan.

TO LIVE IS CHRIST

Day 1 The Surest Way to Unhappiness

> *For to me, to live is Christ and to die is gain.* Philippians 1:21

"I just want to be happy" was Coleen's reply. She smiled as she said it but the words came out with sort of a sigh that betrayed the fact that somehow this happiness had eluded her. The question that she had responded to was the age-old one: "For you, what is the meaning and purpose of life?" For Coleen this was to pursue and gain inner happiness. It is probable that she will never reach her goal. She has started on the wrong road; she has taken aim at a target that will never stay stationary long enough for a direct hit. She will have glances and glimpses of it but as soon as she tries to capture it, happiness will take flight. She has chosen the surest way to unhappiness— she has decided to seek happiness.

Human happiness is not an end but a result. It is not a goal but a by-product. To seek it is to try to have the butter without milking the cow.

There are a few reasons that seeking after your own happiness will result in disaster. The first is that to make yourself happy, at least in the way the majority of people perceive attaining happiness, is to constantly direct your thoughts inward—to always be thinking about yourself above everyone else in order to be happy. (After all, it is our happiness that we are ultimately concerned with, not the happiness of someone else. Happiness for others is secondary, coming only after we have satisfied ourselves.) This, stated simply, is pure selfishness. Not that people who are selfish never do nice things for others—they very frequently do. But the motivation is seldom to simply please the other person but usually to receive some kind of stroke or payoff in return. It is niceness for self-centered reasons. (I'm afraid that even those of us who are trying not to be self-centered find ourselves doing this an embarrassingly large percentage of the time as well.) Thinking about yourself is not the way to happiness but the way to hell. Quite possibly one of the things that will contribute to making hell very miserable is that it will be filled with all of the same kind of creatures—selfish ones.

Trying to make yourself happy is really something that is beyond your ability to do. God has placed in every heart the very longing for this deep inner happiness, but He has placed the satisfaction for it just out of our reach. Rather, it is the homing beacon in our hearts that points to the true source of deep, contented happiness—God Himself.

Write a prescription for true happiness.

Day 2 To Live for Riches

Do not store up for yourselves treasures on earth, where moth and rust destroy, and where thieves break in and steal. Matthew 6:19

Dumps are the graveyards of "things." Bulldozers mercilessly plow under what once were the valuables of a society obsessed with having things. A keen observer can spot the carcasses of what had once been glistening stereos, polished TV sets, and sparkling refrigerators. This is the inevitable resting place of all "things." Undoubtedly, every item in the room where you are sitting will sooner or later find its way to the dump.

The reason, of course, is that all material things lose their value with the passage of time. They decay with age, or, more frequently, break down and cease to function. Because of this fact and others, the pursuit of material things is a revolving door to emptiness.

The insatiable desire to possess more and more has become unquenchable in affluent countries. To feed that desire we have developed an elaborate wall of insulation against the poverty of those less fortunate. For many Christians this insulating wall is built upon rationalization. Many paint their desire to disguise luxuries as "needs" (as in, "I *need* a new $30,000 sports car). Others even go so far as to claim that God wants us to be rich.

The reality is that Jesus put a ceiling on our greed and desire. "But if we have food and clothing, we will be content with that" (1 Tim. 6:8). Christians have been encouraged to seek no more than the basics of living, not the luxuries. This is not to suggest that having something more than food and clothing is particularly evil—after all, God does pour out His blessing on many—but to live for things beyond those necessities is launching upon the most futile of pursuits.

To live for riches is ultimately unsatisfying. It is a thirst that can never be quenched, an investment in things temporary. The dumps and wrecking yards bear mute testimony to the final end of all the great "goodies" that occupy the center of so many existences. In hard contrast stands another investment—one that lasts forever. Making spiritual things the goal of your life may not put a Mercedes in the garage, but it may put another soul into eternity.

For to me, to live in riches is a cotton candy existence—great promise and color but no nutrition or content. Millions settle for it even though there is a full meal in plain sight.

Make a list of all your wants. Circle the things that are really needs.

Day 3 To Live Is Another

> *Man is like a breath; his days are like a fleeting shadow.* Psalm 144:4

Life isn't worth living without him (or her). It's a line that comes bubbling over from daytime soaps. The scene is played with passion as the jilted lover throws herself out of the set window to the imagined death 30 stories below. (Of course, in real life she lands on foam pads two feet from the window sill!)

Most people do not commit suicide at the departure of someone they love. (Although I have known several who actually did.)

A far more common response is a sort of emotional and spiritual despair that can become a slow form of suicide or even a "sentence" of life. In other words, for some the purpose of life is tied so closely to another person that his or her loss or rejection makes life empty, hollow, and meaningless.

While despair and grief are natural and right when one has lost a close person in life, the prolonged form of agony is a signal of a deeper problem. It is the first payoff of a faulty investment—an investment only in others.

Often times it is the later years of life when the futility of making humans the center of our lives comes to fruition. Humans break, they hurt, they disappoint, they die. They can leave the one who has invested in them all alone and abandoned. This becomes especially apparent as one gets older and family and friends fade away. The world is full of many bitter old people who have nothing left to live for because those whom they lived for have vanished.

It is true that people are important. It is true that it is part of God's will that we are concerned about and pour ourselves into the lives of others. But people and our love for them always come after our love for God.

Those who come to feel that their happiness or value is dependent on other people are candidates for a cruel surprise. Even the best men or women are mere shadows of the One who is unfailing and who loves unconditionally. One of the first things that students in lifesaving classes are taught is that they should never allow a drowning person to cling to them. It will ultimately cause the death of both the victim and the rescuer.

Our world is full of drowning people clinging to each other for flotation and yet sinking deeper all the while. Clinging to God will not only allow us to stay above water but to carry others with us as well.

Describe in your own words how you can love people without living for them.

Day 4 For Me to Live Is Fun

> *And he told them this parable: "The ground of a certain rich man produced a good crop. He thought to himself, 'What shall I do? I have no place to store my crops.'*
> *"Then he said, 'This is what I'll do. I will tear down my barns and build bigger ones, and there I will store all my grain and my goods. And I'll say to myself, "You have plenty of good things laid up for many years. Take life easy; eat, drink and be merry."'"* Luke 12:16-19

Nobody likes to be called names. A fat person is not usually referred to as a glutton (even if the fat is from overeating) but rather is referred to as someone who has a weight problem. Lazy people are termed "carefree." Alcoholics think the name "drunk" distasteful; they have the disease of alcoholism.

In the same way, if you accuse someone of being a "hedonist," he or she would likely reply, "No, I'm just a person who likes to have fun." A hedonist is a person who feels that the pursuit of personal pleasure is the chief goal in life. But the word hedonist sounds hard and clinical—almost perverted. Hedonists would prefer the term "fun seeker." This kind of term would give the picture of a glamorous and exciting type of person who always makes things happen, one who jets from here to there and spends carefree time and dollars on the way.

There is another word for the people who describe themselves with the words "all I want to do is have fun"; that word is selfish. Now this is a very nasty word, far worse than hedonist. Nobody wants to be called selfish. But the truth is, pleasure gratification is usually self-centered. It seeks to fill oneself rather than to empty it.

Searching after fun has a few inherent problems. One is that the same old fun can get boring after awhile. Therefore, there is a tendency to always need a bigger and better fix of fun. It is an escalating scale to nowhere. Seeking after fun is usually done at someone else's expense. The old cliché, "Do your own thing as long as you don't hurt anyone," is often invoked on behalf of the pleasure seekers. The problem is that almost everything done has an impact beyond ourselves and our small group of friends. The impact is often negative. What is usually meant by those who throw out that phrase is, "If I can't see the damage done to anyone, it's OK." This way of thinking throws open the door to a host of evil actions and tragic consequences that, though they are not seen on the surface, are no less real. "Many a house is brought down by unseen termites."

Another problem with fun is that it is temporary. It has a short duration. God designed fun to be the accent mark of life, not the bedrock of it. Surprisingly enough, it is the "regular stuff" of life not the pinnacles, that gives the most lasting joy. Joy is the deep quality of inner peace that is like an anchor holding our spirit in place during the roughest of seas. Fun runs out, joy sticks around. Fun is quick, easy, and over in a hurry, often with a horrible price tag. Joy is tougher—more costly up front but worthwhile in the end.

What are some fun things that God has made for you to do? What would be the danger in living for them?

Day 5 To Live Is Aimless

> *You have made known to me the path of life; you will fill me with joy in your presence, with eternal pleasures at your right hand.* Psalm 16:11

It was a smoky coffee shop just outside of London, England. She was an acquaintance of a friend who was taking me around the little hamlet.

Her name was Anne; she had thin, high cheekbones smeared with rouge of such a color that it made her appear corpselike. Her eyes were deep green and seemed to look past you as she talked like she was searching for ghosts in the haze of smoke. As we talked, she continuously played with her cigarette, twirling it in her long, bony fingers. Her appearance was that of a once sleek car now thrashed from the neglect of its owners.

I am still baffled as to why she chose me to pour out her heart to. I was a complete stranger—an American, a foreigner. Perhaps that was why. But the story she told was one of the fast lane going sour.

We talked for hours. She related incident after incident, each of which would have been major catastrophes in the life of any one person, as if they were to her common, everyday events. The drug addiction, the child out of wedlock, the jilted lover, the deep poverty (she survived only by the British form of welfare), the menial jobs, the constant hovering sadness.

Hearing all of this made my heart go out to this pathetic little person. I searched for a way to gently bring up the hope that Christ could offer in her life. "Would you like to change things?" I asked.

Anne ground the butt of her cigarette into the grimy ashtray and hung her hair down to one side. After a long pause, she said, "No, I don't think so."

Walking from the cafe I was stunned that a person could get to the point where life had no meaning or purpose, and where one could be gutted of all will or strength to try to get better. I shouldn't have been surprised. There are people all around us who have realized the aimlessness of chasing after the things that don't satisfy, and they have given up trying, neglecting and rejecting the only One who could actually give meaning and purpose to life.

Think about the empty, vacant eyes and the drifting lives hoping to land on some island of refuge that will sustain them.

In brilliant contrast stands the offer of Christ and the promise of peace and purpose to anyone who will take the challenge. To live for anything else is ultimately aimless.

If you could write a letter to the girl in the true incident above, what would it say?

Day 6 To Die Is Gain

> *Where, O death, is your victory? Where, O death, is
> your sting?* 1 Corinthians 15:55

One of the most infrequent things I used to do as a kid was
to say my prayers.

We had a family who repeated little rhyming or formula
prayers—"Thank you for the birds that sing, thank you God
for everything," for example. But the "killer" prayer in my
book was the old favorite that went, "Now I lay me down to
sleep . . . . " Now that part was OK. In fact, that's exactly what
was happening. I was lying down to get some winks. (I'm still
not sure why I was supposed to inform God of this fact.) The
next part went, "I pray the Lord my soul to keep." Fair enough;
in fact, it might have been a little comforting if it had not been
tied to the next line, which said, "If I should die before I wake
. . . . " Now what kind of talk is that for a six-year-old? From
that point my mind would take off. How would I die before I
woke up? Would the bunk bed collapse and they find me
under a pile of mattresses while my brother slept on soundly?
Would the bogey man finally come and get me (he was out
there, you know)? Would one nuclear bomb ruin my whole
evening? Besides I never thought about dying before, so that
line scared the wits out of me.

The tail ending of the prayer didn't salvage anything: "I
pray the Lord my soul to take." Hey! Wait a minute. I don't
want to go anywhere! I'm only six years old! I'm too young to
die. I don't want to go anywhere. Leave me in my bed! At an
early age it began to dawn on me that death was not a fun
proposition; the older I became the more obvious it was that
death was no friend to me. Then suddenly there comes a passage in God's Word that suggests it might not be so bad. In
fact, it even suggests that it is better than what is here. (This is
based on the assumption that "to live is Christ" is true for the
reader.)

In our society, death is the final taboo. We willingly talk of
the death of others but avoid speaking and thinking with any

seriousness about our own inevitable end. For many, death means the final extinguishing of existence. It is the ultimate and unavoidable bad joke.

For the Christian, there is another perspective altogether. Death is simply a doorway to a realm that makes Disneyland look like a slum.

Spend a few minutes thinking about your own death. What would you like people to say about what you contributed while you were here?

Week Three

CALLED TO SUFFER

Day 1 To Be Like Him

> *Whatever happens, conduct yourselves in a man-*
> *ner worthy of the gospel of Christ. Then, whether I*
> *come and see you or only hear about you in my*
> *absence, I will know that you stand firm in one*
> *spirit, contending as one man for the faith of the*
> *gospel without being frightened in any way by*
> *those who oppose you. This is a sign to them that*
> *they will be destroyed, but that you will be saved—*
> *and that by God. For it has been granted to you on*
> *behalf of Christ not only to believe on him, but also*
> *to suffer for him, since you are going through the*
> *same struggle you saw I had, and now hear that I*
> *still have.* Philippians 1:27-30

So, you want to be like Jesus, eh? You want to be just like Him? You're sure? Wouldn't you rather be like many of His other self-proclaimed followers who pick with care and discrimination which of His teachings they would like to follow? No, huh? Well you realize what you are in for if you really want to be like Him. He will not stop at anything to change and purify you. It may be very painful. You probably won't like it.

Am I trying to discourage you? Well maybe, but only in the sense that I think it is much better for Christianity to have people involved in it who are really willing to be changed. The other kind are what give Christianity most of its credibility problems.

Let me give you an idea of what you are asking for if you want to be like Him.

First of all, get rid of the notion that you will be the strong-leader-of-people-type. All that charisma and power may come to be a part of you but it will be when you are not particularly seeking it—and when you don't care if you have it.

Then recognize that Jesus wants to be more than the miracle man, the wise teacher, the clever thinker or the courageous temple cleanser. You may wish to be like Him in those things, and that is good, but He has far more dimensions than that. If you want to be like Him you will have to suffer like Him. You will have to become like the Christ at Gethsemane, who prayed in agony knowing His life was soon to be painfully ended. You may have to experience betrayal and rejection from those who you think love you most. You may have to have the whole crowd turn on you like a pack of animals. You may find yourself the target for abuse by strangers who simply will use you as a means for venting their anger, frustration, or guilt.

Sound like fun? You bet it's not.

Oh, you want to know why God would let crummy things like that happen to those who love Him? Why does He not protect us like He promises in other parts of the Bible? That's a good question. The only answer I can think of is that for some reason becoming like Christ requires that we experience things very similar to what He experienced. It plows some lines in our character that God can fill with Himself.

So if you have decided that you would rather not be changed in such a dramatic way I wouldn't blame you a bit. But if you think you can pay the price, welcome aboard. We need more hands on this ship. It is the only one that stays afloat in the end.

Create a contract between you and God, offering to follow Him and, if necessary, to suffer for Him.

Day 2 Everybody Pays

> *Therefore, just as sin entered the world through one man, and death through sin, and in this way death came to all men, because all sinned.* Romans 5:12

"OK," said Mrs. Houser, "I want to know who stuck my coffee cup to my desk with super glue."

Naturally, the entire eighth grade class was silent. It was

Mrs. Houser's abrasive personality that invited little pranks like this in the first place. To knowingly acknowledge guilt would be like volunteering to board a train to the Auschwitz concentration camp.

Mrs. Houser's eyes scanned the class, looking for some telltale sign of guilt. She found dozens of them. Actually, this was the first time that most of the students had heard of the prank and their suppressed laughter helped cover the real villain, who was also trying hard to swallow his giggle. "All right," she said, "unless the guilty party comes forward, you shall all have detention tomorrow."

The class was suddenly filled with moans of despair. "But we didn't do it," one of the students sighed.

"It doesn't matter," replied Mrs. Houser. "If I were God, I would know who did this terrible thing; but I'm not so everybody pays!"

Everybody paid the following day, and although some of the kids were a bit put out by the hassle of having to stay after school, most agreed that it was worth it, seeing Ol' Lady Houser trying to pry her ever-present coffee cup from the desk.

In some ways the world is much like Mrs. Houser's class. Somebody does something wrong, and everybody pays. A few careless people forget to put their campfires out and the whole forest burns to the ground. A few rowdy teenagers swipe the mascot from a rival high school so the Board of Education cancels the senior prom. A wacko dictator decides to "push the button," and millions of innocent people evaporate.

It all started with Adam and Eve. They sinned, so everybody pays by the existence of death, suffering, and a host of other problems which plague mankind. The suffering continues with people all around us making wrong choices for which they suffer and we suffer. (If your parents have ever been through a divorce, you know what I mean.) In fact, a host of bad things happen to some very good people because of the "everybody pays" rule in creation.

While this may seem very unfair, we must remember that

God's way of thinking and doing is beyond the horizon of our understanding. He is going to work it all out according to a huge tapestry of fairness and justice. Resist the urge to describe the whole picture based on the one puzzle piece you happen to have.

There are several interesting things about the "everyone pays" rule. In some senses we actually deserve what we are getting. If Adam and Eve hadn't sinned we probably would have done so ourselves. At any rate, most of us, even with our limited number of years on this globe, have contributed plenty to our own misery and to the misery of others.

Though we more or less deserve the "everybody pays" rule, there was Someone who paid who didn't deserve it at all: Jesus Christ. When God put the "everybody pays" rule into effect He included Himself. He paid in the garden, in a Roman courtyard, and on a little hill between the city of Jerusalem and the city dump. When God makes us pay for something that we claim we didn't do, it would be good to remember that He isn't asking us to do what He has never done Himself.

Write a note to God confessing some specific way that you have caused the hurting or suffering of another.

Day 3 False Suffering

Blessed are those who are persecuted because of righteousness, for theirs is the kingdom of heaven.
Blessed are you when people insult you, persecute you and falsely say all kinds of evil against you because of me. Matthew 5:10,11

I'm sure that to this day Eddie Fiedler thinks that he was suffering for Jesus through high school. He probably wears the abuse he received like a badge of honor. I don't think there is any doubt that he suffered through high school. I think there is great doubt that he suffered for Jesus.

First of all, Eddie was pretty much of a geek. He wore clothes that were a few years out of style because he thought they were in style. This is not particularly good or bad, but it does set you up for ridicule whether you believe in Jesus or not. Somewhere along the line Eddie graduated to polyester and rayon. If he got too close to a heater his clothes began to melt.

Eddie suffered for other things besides his appearance. He suffered for his self-righteousness. It was not that his choices were intrinsically bad; in fact, some of them were very wise and good. But it was the obnoxious way that he let you know about them. "Hey Eddie, seen any good movies lately?" might be responded to by the twisted up expression of pride and a slow but distinct response of, "I don't care to waste my time being influenced by the trash they show at movies." And this statement was always made in such a way as to make the one who asked the question feel just a little lower than bathroom scum.

Eddie suffered because he represented religion to everybody, but not particularly Christianity. He refused to associate with those of questionable values. He made little gestures of disgust and jabbing comments when thrust into conversation where "untouchables" might be involved. In return, the untouchables (a vast majority) designated him as the jerk of the school and treated him as such.

Eventually Eddie transferred to a Christian school, complaining about the persecution and suffering he endured for trying to be like Jesus. It would have been a noble thing if it were true. Unfortunately, Eddie suffered not because he was so much like Jesus but because he was too little like Him.

Make a list of the things for which a Christian your age might genuinely suffer.

Day 4 One Fine Day on a Hillside

> *"O house of Israel, can I not do with you as this pot-*
> *ter does?" declares the Lord. "Like clay in the hand*
> *of the potter, so are you in my hand, O house of*
> *Israel."* Jeremiah 18:6

Imagine that a rock could think. Imagine that there is one particular rock, happily at home with all of the other rocks in his little hillside.

One day a group of men began to dig into the hillside; one by one they crumbled or took away all of his friends. He screamed in silent agony as they cut away his supports and wrenched him away from the security of his hill and cast him down the slope. He wailed without sound as they hoisted him to the wagon and carted him into the city.

For awhile he was placed alongside fellow rocks of similar make and texture. He began to feel secure. Then one day a dark-haired man with strong hands singled him out and had him carried to what the rock could only describe as a torture chamber.

There were pieces of his friends lying about the room, and the instruments of their destruction were resting neatly on a solitary table. The rock was placed in the middle of the room. It was to be a public humiliation.

Before long the dark-haired man came into the room and snatched up the tools—a hammer and chisel. He strolled over to the rock, eyed the slab for a moment, and then violently struck off a sizable outcropping of the stone. The rock moaned in agony. "That was a distinct part of my personality!" cried the rock to himself. "And now it is gone forever. What will make me unique from other rocks?"

Of course the workman had no idea of the thoughts that bounced through the molecules of that particular stone. All the stone knew was that he was in great pain. With every swing of the hammer little bits of himself exploded away. "I always thought of myself as a tower of strength," whined the rock, "but who would want to look at me now?" Still the dark-haired man pounded and chiseled relentlessly. Before long he began to use abrasive tools to remove particles of the stone. The poor rock was in complete misery. "This is my darkest hour," thought the stone. "I'm undone, worthless—a nothing. Oh, I wish I could have stayed in my hillside forever."

If the dark-haired man had any inkling of these thoughts he never gave any indication. One day he laid down his tools and stepped back to survey what he had done. The rock looked at chunks of himself scattered about the workshop floor and wished that he could squeeze out at least one stony tear. "I have no future now," thought the stone. "I have been stripped of my importance and strength."

Suddenly the dark-haired man was not alone. The visitor gasped audibly and stared open-mouthed at the stone. "What do you call it?" asked the newcomer.

The dark-haired man was silent for a moment and then softly replied, "David. I call it David."

What are some of the things that God is trying to chip out of your life?

Day 5 The Final Calling

> *I am sending you out like sheep among wolves. Therefore be as shrewd as snakes and as innocent as doves. But be on your guard against men; they will hand you over to the local councils and flog you in their synagogues. On my account you will be brought before governors and kings as witnesses to them and to the Gentiles.*
> Matthew 10:16-18

Some of the most haunting accounts of man's cruelty and barbarism to his fellow man can be found in the ancient accounts of the persecution of early Christians.

Although just a handful of the thousands of brave martyrdoms have been recorded and preserved, they give a picture of the kind of earthshaking force that changed the face of the world. A few of these accounts are so detailed that they give a wonderful picture of the kind of inner quality and Christlikeness that eventually overcame the most powerful government known to earth—without the use of a sword.

One of these reflectors of God's love was a man called Laurentius (often referred to as Saint Laurence).

In the year A.D. 257 trouble began to erupt for the Christians in Rome after a few years of relative growth and calm. The Roman Emperor Valerian was persuaded to begin a purge of all Christians. The bishop of the church of Rome was immediately apprehended and put to death. Laurentius, the principle deacon of the church, moved quickly to distribute the funds from the church treasury to the hands of the most needy in order to keep the money from being confiscated by the Roman government.

When word of the distribution reached the emperor he immediately demanded that Laurentius give an account of the church treasures at the royal court.

The humble deacon promised to satisfy this request. With a great deal of trouble he gathered together a huge number of the aged, helpless, sick, and poverty-stricken people and brought them before the emperor. Laurentius then approached the mighty emperor, who sprang to his feet and demanded to know the whereabouts of the church treasure. The man of God held out his hand in the direction of the decrepit masses and said, "These, these are the true treasures of the church."

In August of A.D. 258, Laurentius was whipped with iron rods, sat upon a wooden horse, and had his limbs dislocated. Finally, he was placed upon a large grill to be slowly burned alive. Witnesses recorded that this man went to his death cheerfully and calmly, committing himself to the Almighty.

While it is doubtful that many of us will encounter the kind of persecution that came upon the early Christians (and which is still occurring in some countries) it is important to remember that we have been guaranteed a heritage of persecution, not one of ease. It is the salt that causes a wound to sting, not the salve. God's people will suffer persecution because they act as His agent of salt in a wounded world. In fact, if we are not a royal pain to those who do not know Christ, we may need to examine our own sense of priorities to see if we have worn off the points of friction.

How might a person from your society or culture be persecuted?

Day 6 The Bubble People

If the world hates you, keep in mind that it hated me first. John 15:18

If there were a land where the inhabitants were made of bubbles, you can be sure that there would be one thing missing from that place—points.

Bubble people would not like points or sharp edges. They would only favor round, soft edges to come up against. Bubble people would not like those who armed themselves with pointed objects. They would be afraid that someone would come and start bursting the various bubbles that comprised their lives. If they knew of a person who played with pointed things they would certainly avoid him, especially if he had popped a few bubbles intentionally or even accidentally.

To many people, Christians are the "keepers of the points" in a world full of bubble people. The ideas of Christ prick and deflate the swelled-up pretensions of many. His truth is solid, real, and sharp. Bubble people live in a world largely made up of fancy pipe dreams and elaborately fashioned bits of soap that have zero content.

Bubble people do not have to remain bubble people. When Christ gets a hold of them He begins to burst the bubbles that once were so sacred, and to develop in their place a people who are real, firm, solid—even a little pointed. Suddenly, bubble people do not like them anymore.

Bubble people will go to great lengths to avoid those who are gradually becoming solid or gripping pointed principles. They will often accuse them of narrowness (what can one expect when one starts to become pointed?), hypocrisy and the like.

Pointed people are to be excluded, ridiculed, harassed, maligned, blackballed, or cajoled into breaking off or compromising their points. It should not be surprising to us when we are disliked for being Christians. People don't like to have their bubbles popped. In fact, if we are liked too much by the bubble people around us, it may be a good time to stop and see just how solid and pointed we really are.

What are some of the "points" in a Christian life that might make a non-Christian uncomfortable? Why?

Week Four

THE NEEDS OF OTHERS

Day 1 United We Stand

> *If you have any encouragement from being united with Christ, if any comfort from his love, if any fellowship with the Spirit, if any tenderness and compassion, then make my joy complete by being like-minded, having the same love, being one in spirit and purpose. Do nothing out of selfish ambition or vain conceit, but in humility consider others better than yourselves. Each of you should look not only to your own interests, but also to the interests of others.* Philippians 2:1-4

When I was a kid we used to play a game called Red Rover. A group of kids would link arms and call to another much larger group, "Red Rover, Red Rover, let Janie (or whoever) come over."

At that chant the kid whose name was called would make a charge toward the line of interlocked youngsters and try to break through. If the kid succeeded he or she got to go back to the large group for another try. If the attempt failed the kid had to link up with the smaller group. Eventually everyone in the larger group would be caught, leaving the last person to break through to be the winner.

Naturally the kids in the large group wanted to win the game and would use some good strategy to keep from being caught. They would spot the smallest or weakest kids in the chain and would charge through their locked arms with a roar. Naturally, the little or frail kids would loosen their grip before some monster hit them so they would not suffer a snapped arm.

The kids on the defensive team had strategy as well. They would wedge the little guys between two beefy co-students and count on the larger kids to hold onto the limbs of the little ones if they started to chicken out.

The game did get a bit rough but to my recollection no arms were ever broken (although a few were certainly stretched to their limits).

Christians are called to link together. They are asked to be of one mind and purpose—to share the same love for the Master and the same respect for each other.

This should come naturally. We have a common adversary who is looking to break through our lines at any place he can. Unfortunately, many Christians are divided to such a degree that they will not even speak to each other, let alone link up with each other. Satan does not have to break through our lines at all. He simply walks through.

Sometimes the divisions are along party lines: "My church is better than your church." Sometimes the divisions exist because of the exclusiveness of one of the bodies: "We have something you don't have." All of the divisions are tragic.

Interlocking is not the only thing that we have been called to do. We are called to look out for the interests of each other—especially the weaker and younger ones around us. We are to hang on to them to protect them, to encourage them when things look tough.

Locking together, hanging on to each other, protecting the weaker ones, watching for our points of vulnerability and covering for them. These are high ideas. God would not ask us to do them if they could not be realities.

Is there someone in your youth group or church who will support you when things are tough? Who? Who do you hold up?

Day 2 Love and Limits

> And you have forgotten that word of encourage-
> ment that addresses you as sons: "My son, do not
> make light of the Lord's discipline, and do not lose
> heart when he rebukes you, because the Lord dis-
> ciplines those he loves, and he punishes everyone
> he accepts as a son."
> Endure hardship as discipline; God is treating
> you as sons. For what son is not disciplined by his
> father? Hebrews 12:5-7

One of the great fears that is expressed when a person begins to deal with such concepts as loving your neighbor as yourself and going the extra mile is that of becoming a doormat or someone's patsy.

No one wants to be used and discarded by cruel or greedy people. Nobody wants to be taken advantage of. God does not want that either.

Sometimes doing what is best for someone is not the same as doing what pleases someone.

One day two young brothers decided to dig to China in a small corner of a yet undeveloped backyard. As the grade school explorers headed towards "China" they found the going a bit difficult, so they decided to stop and create a "foxhole fort" about three feet deep.

In order to have a "legitimate" fort they had to scrounge up any bits of discarded lumber, tree branches, or old building material they could find. The former explorers turned general contractors decided that they must become pioneers.

The brothers prowled the gullies and trash dumpsters for decent raw materials to build their fort. It was during this process that the oldest of the pair firmly planted his foot on a rusty nail protruding from an old plank he was trying to liberate.

The boy howled in pain and yanked his foot from the projectile. Immediately blood began to fill his tennis shoe. He limped home in agony, tears welling in his eyes.

The boy's father could hear his sobbing cries as he turned the corner onto the front walk. Dad dropped his paper and opened the front door in time to be greeted by the grubby, tear-lined face of his eldest son.

In a few moments the father had the boy perched awkwardly on the bathtub rim as he carefully cleaned out the wound. "I'm afraid that I'm going to have to take you in for a tetanus shot," said the father gently.

The boy burst into tears. "No! No shots!" he cried.

"I'm sorry, son," said the father, "but we don't have a choice. If you don't get a shot you run the risk of infection and maybe worse."

The boy protested and cried even more bitterly. "I'd rather die than get a shot," he screamed. But it was to no avail. The father was not about to let him run the risk of illness just because the boy feared a needle in the hind end.

A few hours later the visit to the doctor was over. The boy sat leaning to one side, grumpily nursing a grape sucker the doctor had given him for being brave (well, sort of brave).

What he had received was painful, humiliating, and the "end process" of his father's love. It was doing what the boy needed even if he didn't understand, rather than doing what the boy wanted.

It is not too difficult to see that we can do the same. In fact, in our love for others we must sometimes do what is the best for those we love even if they don't realize it themselves.

Can you think of a time you had to say no to a request because you loved a person? What was it?

Day 3 A Sweet Word

Pleasant words are a honeycomb, sweet to the soul and healing to the bones. Proverbs 16:24

Think about a person who means a great deal to you—a person who encourages you and makes you feel important.

It is a good bet that the person you are thinking about means a lot to you because he or she honestly communicates his or her positive thoughts about you directly to you.

Everyone needs some sort of affirmation. Some people do very silly things to get it. Some make fools of themselves. Children who do not get positive affirmation or attention will often do something rotten to at least get some kind of notice, even if it is negative.

Most of us not only realize that we need affirmation but we love to receive it (if it is genuine, of course). We like to have our strong points recognized and we enjoy having worth in the eyes of someone else. If we can see how much we enjoy honest affirmation it should be clear to us that others must need this kind of recognition as well.

Pleasant words come in here. Sweet to say, sweet to hear, and healthy for the souls of both giver and receiver. Kind, thoughtful words can be soothing and uplifting. Being a person who looks for things to affirm in our friends and family should become part of our Christian habit.

Sweet words also act as agents of peace, as cement to bond together relationships that have been damaged or broken. They contribute to the unity and wholeness of a Christian group, just as backbiting and gossip contribute to the deterioration of a Christian group.

Sweet words must also be true words. There is no point in fabricating a web of deception with our tongue in order to make people feel good about something that they should feel bad about. Sweet words can point out even the most painful truth in a way that is calming and caring.

Sweet words are in the best interest of everyone. Can you imagine an argument or disagreement that is normally carried out at a high decibel level being conducted with kindness and gently-thought-out words? It would probably not solve the point of disagreement but it would make the process of coming to a conclusion much less painful.

Sweet words come from a sweet spirit. They are available in direct proportion to the amount of control we give the Holy Spirit in our lives.

We all love sweet words when we hear them. It's even better to be the one who gives them.

Keep track of the spirit of your conversations today. How much sweetness or affirmation was there? What would you want to change about the way you talk to people?

Day 4 Nothing Expected

> *If you love those who love you, what credit is that to you? Even "sinners" love those who love them. And if you do good to those who are good to you, what credit is that to you? Even "sinners" do that. And if you lend to those from whom you expect repayment, what credit is that to you? Even "sinners" lend to "sinners," expecting to be repaid in full.* Luke 6:32-34

It was just a few weeks before Christmas and Jeff had managed to scrape enough money together from his allowance at home and from his part-time job at the pizza house to get a special gift for each of the people in his family and for his girlfriend Belinda.

Christmas always used to make him feel a little guilty because his gifts were somewhere a step above the old plaster cast of hands that he used to make in school and give to his folks. In fact, his mother loved the plaster hand casts and has a wall in the hallway dedicated to them.

This year it would be different. He actually had money to spend. Jeff propped himself up in his bed and went down the list of goodies that he had bought. "I hope Mom will be happy with the perfume I bought her," he thought. "I don't know if it's her flavor or if she will ever even use it, though," he mused. (Jeff's mom always told him that she expected nothing but his love for a present.)

This would be the third Christmas since Jeff's dad left and Jeff sometimes felt that his mom needed to get on with life and find another husband. That was the real reason for the perfume.

Jeff got out all of the gifts and lined them up on the counter. The transformable toy for his younger brother was small but hard to find. The record albums of the gooney group that his junior high sister liked so much were an embarrassment for him to even buy. (He made sure to tell the checkout person that the albums were a gift for his "dwid" little sister. The necklace for Belinda ought to make her know that she's special to him, but it was the bottle of perfume for his mom that troubled him. He sat in his bed and stared at the box. The more he thought about it the more he wasn't sure about the gift. It might bring back all of the old memories of the "good ol' Christmases." It might be taken wrong. It might uncork things that would be sad or unpleasant. Even if it didn't, it might not be her fragrance.

Jeff dug out the receipt and took the perfume back to the store. Then he called Pastor John at the church.

That Christmas morning Jeff's mom opened a small, flat gift with her name on it. The card read: "Dear Mom, For Christmas this year I gave a Christmas tree to the Mansfield family because Pastor John said they could not afford one. I left it anonymously on their doorstep but I really gave it as a gift from you. Love, Jeff."

At the bottom of the small, flat package was a plaster dish with the imprints of two rather large hands and the name Jeff scrawled in them.

Can you think of someone who needs a simple gift of love from you?

Day 5 Carry Me

> *We who are strong ought to bear with the failings of the weak and not to please ourselves. Each of us should please his neighbor for his good, to build him up. For even Christ did not please himself but, as it is written: "The insults of those who insult you have fallen on me."* Romans 15:1-3

"I don't see any needs in our church," remarked Allison. "Everyone seems to be doing fine."

"Do you know *everyone*?" asked the youth worker.

"I know most of them," shot back Allison. "If there were

some real needs I'd be willing to pitch in and help."

"Perhaps I could get you to do an assignment," said the young man. "Pick somebody you don't know from that crowd of people over there."

"Right now?" asked Allison.

"Sure," her friend replied.

"OK. The little old lady with the purple dress and the bun in her hair," said Allison. "What's the assignment?"

"I want you to try and get to know that lady. Her name is Virginia Green, and I want you to come back to class and report on any needs she might have. If she has none, tell us that as well."

"How long do I have?" asked Allison.

"How about a week?" responded the youth man.

"All right, you've got a deal."

Allison was a brash and bold young lady. She marched over to Mrs. Green and asked if she could interview her for a report that she was asked to give on people in the church.

Mrs. Green was a little shocked at the sudden attention but warmed to the idea. The interview was set for the following Thursday at Mrs. Green's little cottage in the old part of town.

Allison showed up at the appointed time on Thursday and was ushered into a cozy little home that had the distinct smell of "grandma" about it. She sat in an old rocker with doilies on the arms, and got comfortable to begin the interview. Mrs. Green surprised her by initiating the conversation.

"That rocker has seen quite a few babies being raised on it," she said. "I have four sons and one daughter, but none of them live in town; not much work here, you know." Allison could detect a hint of sadness in her voice from the way she said that.

As the conversation progressed Allison discovered that Mrs. Green was a widow who had lost two of her sons in World War II. She lived on a pension and suffered from terrible bouts of arthritis. She did not complain about this but asked for Allison's help in opening a jar that her deformed hands could not grip.

She seemed to have a deep and fervent faith and had

served the church loyally for many years as a Sunday School teacher.

Allison was fascinated and touched at the same time. She overstayed her time by at least an hour.

The following Sunday morning Allison stood to read her report on the needs of people in the church. The gist of what it said is best summed up by her closing line. "I once thought that if I didn't see a need that it did not exist. Mrs. Green has shown me that she is in need of someone who will be a friend, who will open her jars and maybe do some light housework. If any of you would like to help, just ask me. But if none of you want to help, it doesn't matter. I'm going to visit Mrs. Green every week."

Try making a report on someone in your church; see what needs he or she has.

Day 6 A Bit of a Prod

And let us consider how we may spur one another
on toward love and good deeds. Hebrews 10:24

We were doing something stupid again! This time it was crawling along the rocky shoreline for fun and adventure and to see what weird things we could pick up from the tide pools.

Eleven-year-olds can make an adventure out of just about anything. The three of us had made quite a bit of distance and collected some great treasures (I had a good-sized sea urchin) when we realized that the tide was coming in and we needed to hurry back.

Unfortunately, we had overspent our time, for high tide was quickly closing in on us and there was only one way back: a narrow rocky ledge that ran along the face of the cliff about 15 feet above the water.

Traveling during low tide, we had walked brazenly over the exposed reef beds and out onto a narrow rock peninsula that housed our newfound treasure. The incoming tide made the same route impossible. We were left with two options: swim (cold and impossible) or take the high road. We chose the high road.

Dennis was small and surefooted. He took the lead, picking the path and calling back warnings about loose or slippery rocks. Keith followed Dennis with a great deal of hesitation. In fact, Keith often didn't want to move at all.

The tide was moving up quickly and soon the waves would be pounding against the sea wall, making the ledge slippery and dangerous. A giant wave could even wash over the little pathway and send us into the drink. Dennis moved as quickly as his goatlike legs would carry him. My progress was impeded by Keith the slug moving slowly and cautiously along the cliff face.

"Hurry up, Keith!" I cried. "We're going to get nailed if you don't!"

"I'm going as fast as I can," he replied in a voice that quivered with fear. I did not believe that he was at top speed but I trudged along, mumbling under my breath until a large wave shattered the cliff face just behind me.

At that point I decided that it was time for action. I reached into the bag that I carried and pulled out the spiny sea urchin. I held the creature at arm's length and yelled to Keith. "You've got a choice. You can either walk at my pace or get this puppy stuck in your rear!"

Keith might have thought I was kidding at first but the look on my face dispelled that idea. He moved.

The urchin came perilously close to its mark that afternoon but it never connected. It didn't have to. Keith quickened his pace and saved both of us from a cold and dangerous swim. Sometimes, being a friend means that you have to do a little prodding for the good of another.

Can you think of anyone who you could lovingly prod towards good? Do you need prodding yourself?

Week Five

THE ATTITUDE OF CHRIST

Day 1 Humility

> *Your attitude should be the same as that of Christ Jesus:*
>
> *Who, being in very nature God, did not consider equality with God something to be grasped, but made himself nothing, taking the very nature of a servant, being made in human likeness. And being found in appearance as a man, he humbled himself and became obedient to death—even death on a cross! Therefore God exalted him to the highest place and gave him the name that is above every name, that at the name of Jesus every knee should bow, in heaven and on earth and under the earth, and every tongue confess that Jesus Christ is Lord, to the glory of God the Father.* Philippians 2:5-11

C.S. Lewis once said, "If you meet a really humble man he will not be what most people call 'humble' nowadays: he will not be a sort of greasy, smarmy person, who is always telling you that, of course, he is nobody. Probably all you will think about him is that he seemed a cheerful, intelligent chap who took a real interest in what YOU said to him. If you do dislike him it will be because you feel a little envious of anyone who seems to enjoy life so easily. He will not be thinking about humility: he will not be thinking about himself at all."[1]

Great thinkers of all ages, when discussing humility, seem to come up with the same basic conclusion; humility begins when we empty ourselves and invest in others.

This is an easy concept to repeat but a far more difficult one to grasp and live out. That is one reason Paul, in writing to the Philippians, gives the example of Christ as our model for humility. He emptied Himself and became interested and involved in the lives of men and women. He listened, He cried, He laughed with His own creation. He even took the job of a thankless servant and washed His followers' feet. Somehow, when people were around Him they sensed that He cared for them and loved them.

It is precisely this investment in others that creates in us a spirit of humility. We become so involved in thinking and caring about God and others that we just don't have time to think about ourselves. This is not something that we can do effortlessly. It takes thought and determination as well as desire. (There are many kind deeds that are done only in the *mind* of a potential doer.)

For some, to forget about themselves is completely out of the question. They are in the world for a limited amount of time and they intend to grab all the gusto they can. Besides, they have their dignity (which has only made them restless and discontent all of their lives) and see themselves as people to be served and catered to. This kind of thinking produces a kind of inner bankruptcy—a cannibalism of one's own soul. A person created by God with the capacity to be larger than life, and solid with the reality of His presence, instead becomes a warped, tiny, ghostlike creature.

The place to start in taking on the attitude of Christ is to realize that we actually are self-centered and proud. It is a difficult thing to admit, but we cannot proceed until we have done it. Once we have faced our true selves in the mirror, we can begin to change what we see. As long as we allow no mirrors in our house, becoming like Him will be impossible.

Can you think of a person who has true humility? What is there about that person that you could imitate?

Footnote
1. Lewis, C.S. *Mere Christianity*. New York: MacMillan, 1952, p. 99.

Day 2 Grubby Love

> Then the righteous will answer him, "Lord, when
> did we see you hungry and feed you, or thirsty and
> give you something to drink?" Matthew 25:37

The dump in Tijuana, Mexico, is not a fun place. As far as dumps go, it is very low-grade trash. Clouds of black smoke billow from the mounds of old tires. The pungent odor mixes with the smell of diesel and the roar of dilapidated trash trucks.

People live here. They build homes out of the refuse of others. The trash heaps are alive with the blackened children scrounging through stomach-turning stench to find the "gold" of the dump people: bits of metal that can be collected and sold for pennies at recycling centers. Others scratch for the remains of edible food to provide for their family or to quench their own gnawing hunger. Illness and despair are constant companions among the people living in the little village constructed of old cardboard boxes.

Every week a small caravan of cars can be seen creating a ribbon of pale smoke as they wind down the dusty hillside to the dump below.

Out of the cars and vans pour a collection of well-scrubbed "gringos," many of whom are "styling" in the latest and most expensive casual wear. They are one of the hundreds of church groups that team up with a guide who regularly ministers to the dump people. Here for just the day, most of them genuinely wanted to help poor people in some way. Now that they stand among the sights and smells of real poverty, they obviously feel some strong misgivings.

Children pour out of the trash piles. They know that this weekly visit would mean a chance for a bath in the portable tub the ministering group always brings with them. (It's a strange contraption fashioned out of an old tent-trailer with fiber glass bottoms and sides.) But the real draw is the bounty of fruit and food that is handed out to those kids who have their weekly baths. The only real drawback of the portable tub is that, with the children of the dump, the last ones often come out dirtier than they go in.

During the visit, sores are treated, medicine distributed, and construction done on the cardboard homes. Really fortunate people have homes made from old scraps of sheet metal and used plywood. Building can be done by any junior carpenter without a permit. The only qualification that matters is that the structure remain standing.

But the real thing that is given is love. Grubby love. Many of the high school students dirty themselves by holding, carrying, and hugging "the least of these." Unfortunately, not everyone who comes has the same feeling. A few of the kids are so shocked by what they see and smell, and so afraid of contaminating their sterile, perfumed bodies and costly clothes, that they creep back into the vehicles. There they sit with their Walkmans on, trying to drown out the realities outside.

Meanwhile, their churchmates find that there is great joy in getting down on their knees in the filth of a Tijuana dump to hold, carry, and hug Jesus Himself.

Who is poor or hurting in your community? What could you do to show Christ's love?

Day 3 The Place God Lives

> For this is what the high and lofty One says—he who lives forever, whose name is holy: "I live in a high and holy place, but also with him who is contrite and lowly in spirit, to revive the spirit of the lowly and to revive the heart of the contrite." Isaiah 57:15

Where does God live? As a kid I figured that He lived on top of a fluffy, white cloud (see what one too many Saturday morning cartoons will do to you?). Of course, I also thought that clouds were made of soft, cottonlike stuff that you could bounce on or dive into.

When I got older I heard someone say that God lived in everything. That sounded pretty good. I could imagine a benevolent force inhabiting crashing waves or majestic peaks. But I was sure that there were some places that God didn't dwell. In cockroaches, for example. In liver, in mosquitos, and definitely not in a certain math teacher I had. The God I had in mind wouldn't be caught dead within 50 feet of her, let alone live in her. As you can sense, even in my adaptation of this idea (which comes from Eastern religions) I was very selective. But when God is merely a force in your thinking you don't honestly expect to find Him when you split open a pineapple.

After becoming a Christian I stumbled upon the verse from Isaiah—57:15, to be exact. I couldn't figure out the way that God inhabits eternity. It is one of those ideas that you understand and don't understand at the same time. In fact, the harder you try to think of God surrounding eternity and time, the quicker the "tilt" signs go on in your head.

But I could, at least in some ways, understand that it is in exclusive people that God will dwell—in those who humble themselves before Him.

What is it like to have God dwell in you? Explaining that is very difficult. It is very much like trying to describe the taste of an orange to someone who has never eaten citrus fruit. You can get a vague idea of the sweet and sour but it falls far short of experience.

It is often suggested that God will not dwell where He is not welcome. He always comes in to live as a king and ruler, not as a guest. If the throne room of our lives is occupied by any other, God will not enter. True spiritual humility chases the impostor from the throne and invites its rightful owner to take His place there.

If you would like to see the dwelling place of God, find a humble heart. Better still, by humbling our own rebellious spirit we provide God a resting place He will not resist.

Write a prayer to God in which you ask Him to be the ruler of your life and to live in you.

Day 4 New Clothes

> *Young men, in the same way be submissive to those who are older. Clothe yourselves with humility toward one another, because, "God opposes the proud but gives grace to the humble."*

Humble yourselves, therefore, under God's mighty hand, that he may lift you up in due time.
1 Peter 5:5,6

Have you ever noticed that for many people the clothes they wear are not so much selected for the comfort or durability that the garment will provide but for the statement that it will make? When this takes place the clothing ceases to be mere clothing but becomes instead a costume.

It has been my observation that there are more costumes worn to the average high school each day than there are clothes. Not that costumes don't serve some of the same functions as clothing: they are made of material, they give warmth and covering; but unlike plain clothing, they also give a message.

We select our costumes based on the image that we would like to project to those around us. Perhaps we want to show that we are the rough and rowdy cowboy type, or the new wave styler, the clone of some current rocker, the super jock, the high fashion woman, or Mr. GQ—even the pencilneck geek or some other countless variation of an image or lifestyle that we want to identify with. (Of course there are those who just wear what their mothers lay out for them, but they are a whole different story.)

Costuming ourselves is not new to mankind. People have always worn various forms of dress to designate their position, philosophy, or belief.

Most of the costuming done in our society is harmless— even a little silly. But some costuming is designed especially to give the appearance of power or authority, even terror (the black-shirted Nazi SS troops with their death's-head insignias, for example).

Often, the message of clothes is "I'm better" or "I have more style and class" or "I have bucks—just look at my labels."

Peter asks the Christian community to put on a new set of clothes. His implication is that we are to change our costumes or the images we are trying to project.

Instead of constantly trying to show off or win a game of one-upmanship, we are asked to take on a different attitude—the attitude of a person who is submissive, teachable, caring, and thoughtful of the ideas and hurts of others.

What God is after is a costume change in our minds. Instead of seeing ourselves as a member of royalty, one to be courted and served by others, we are to see ourselves as one of the servants waiting to be of service to another. Instead of seeing ourselves dressed in the clothes of a dictator we are to see ourselves attired as the poorest of the kingdom.

This does not mean that we think we are insignificant or do not matter at all, for we are all very significant and matter a great deal to God. We are to see in others that same significance and rank that we would ascribe to ourselves—in fact, we should go a bit further and give others a bit more rank than we have. They are corporals and we are privates.

The new clothes have little to do with the ones that we actually wear to school each day, a thought that may have a great deal to do with the attitude that we have while wearing our particular costume. In fact, the new clothes that we are asked to wear are not really new at all. They have had a previous owner. They come to us with bloodstain and sweat from the last time they were worn—on their way to a place called Calvary.

What new attitude would you like to develop this week? Do you look down on anyone because of his or her costume? How do you think that God would want you to treat that person?

Day 5 A Sad but True Tale

You call me "Teacher" and "Lord," and rightly so, for that is what I am. Now that I, your Lord and Teacher, have washed your feet, you also should wash one another's feet. I have set you an example that you should do as I have done for you.
John 13:13-15

Public celebrities pay a big price for their notoriety. Many of them cannot travel without the stares and hassle of star-struck people. Many of them travel with bodyguards, hide out in exclusive clubs, and ride around in limos with the windows blacked out. In some ways, their glamor is also a prison—a prison that thousands are trying to break into.

Beneath real celebrities is a class of people that range from "wanna be's" to those who are paying their dues and are bound for eventual notoriety.

Generally, Christians are not considered in the same league as those with secular celebrity status. There are few genuine believers at the top of the world's heap.

Occasionally we hear of those who picture the big time as their calling from God. Stars for Jesus. People who get so caught up in the machine that makes for notoriety that they forget the heart of the gospel that they claim to serve.

Such was the case of a "rising star" evangelist who happened to be coming to town.

He was a big man with a deep, booming voice. He gripped the pulpit and called on people to commit their lives to Christ. And they did. By the hundreds. His first tour through the area had been well-received. Now he was coming back. The local churches braced together in a rare display of unity to help the week-long crusade happen.

The next Billy Graham is what they called him. The big hall was rented and the publicity completed. The big man would arrive at the airport that evening. One of our group was assigned the job of picking him up and taking him to his hotel room. A wonderful opportunity to spend a little time with a man that God was starting to use in a big way.

The person assigned to pick up the evangelist was waiting for him as he emerged from the plane. She greeted him and carried his luggage to her car, a humble VW beetle.

Suddenly the man balked. "You don't expect ME to ride in THAT, do you?" he asked. The poor courier looked around in amazement, thinking that perhaps her car had been replaced with a rickshaw.

"Well, it's the only car I have," apologized the girl.

"It won't do," roared the evangelist indignantly. "Tell them to send another car or I'll get right back on the airplane; I won't ride in a little death trap!" stormed the man.

The young lady went to the phone booth and explained the problem to the shocked co-workers. They sent another "nicer" car.

The evangelist did his routine. People came forward. We wondered about this until someone reminded us that God even used a donkey once to get his message across.

Rather than break into the Christian celebrity world, this rising star faded out. I have not heard anything about him for years. Things might have been different for him if he had followed the humble example of the One he preached about every night.

What would you have said if you were the owner of the VW beetle?

Day 6 A Long Stride

> *To this you were called, because Christ suffered for you, leaving you an example, that you should follow in his steps.*
>
> *"He committed no sin, and no deceit was found in his mouth."*
>
> *When they hurled their insults at him, he did not retaliate; when he suffered, he made no threats. Instead, he entrusted himself to him who judges justly.* 1 Peter 2:21-23

When I was a little boy, our family went on a walk along the beach. There was plenty of adventure along the high tide line. Huge kelp roots that were the favorite hiding places of small octopi often washed ashore. A kid could rip into them and come out with a creature guaranteed to make his kid sisters squeal in fright. Once in a while a dead shark or jellyfish would wind up on the sand. All of the kids would stand around and poke them with sticks. Along the wet sand, little V-shaped antennas could be seen in the retreating surf, a dead giveaway that little sandcrabs could be scooped up by the handful.

Parents never seemed as interested in all the diversions as the kids were, so it was not uncommon to look up and see them quite a few yards away, their footprints still drawing water in the damp sand. This presented us with another game. Try to stay in the outline of Dad's footprint. First kid to fall out was dead, eaten by killer whales.

His strides were long, our legs were short. It was tricky to hop into each of the wet impressions without losing balance and flopping onto the damp sand. Even though it was a game we played it with dead seriousness. Nobody wanted to be eaten first.

It must have been quite a sight. A ragtag bunch of kids leaping down the sealine, clumsily trying to land in a place that was not created by them and that was way out of their natural step.

The game was not possible to sustain for long. Everyone eventually failed to land squarely in Dad's footsteps. But when we failed we got a new life (which is standard fare in children's games).

The parallel is clear. We are asked to follow Christ's footsteps, which are then described as being perfect in action, speech, and thought. Quite a leap still, I'm afraid. I know I can't always hit the target dead on. But I will take the challenge seriously. There are no killer whales to eat me if I fall, but if I do not get up and play the game some more I will surely be devoured by another enemy. I will look awkward too. It is not my natural step. It is bigger than I am. I have to leap at each step. It takes effort.

But someday, with lots of practice and growth, maybe I'll grow big enough to step into those footsteps with ease. Someday.

What is the hardest thing about the Christian life for you? Make it a point of prayer and practice.

What do you do when you fall down in your Christian life?

GLOW IN THE DARK

Day 1 Candid Christian

> *Therefore, my dear friends, as you have always obeyed—not only in my presence, but now much more in my absence—continue to work out your salvation with fear and trembling, for it is God who works in you to will and to act according to his good purpose.*
>
> *Do everything without complaining or arguing, so that you may become blameless and pure, children of God without fault in a crooked and depraved generation, in which you shine like stars in the universe as you hold out the word of life—in order that I may boast on the day of Christ that I did not run or labor for nothing.* Philippians 2:12-16

Smile! You're on "Candid Camera"!

Those were the opening words to an ancient TV show that featured real people getting fooled by wacky stunts and being filmed, without their knowledge, in various stages of reaction.

People across the nation would roll with laughter at the mailbox that would reject the mail placed into it or the guy changing into Superman in a phone booth—and at the astonished expressions of those captured on film.

The program ended with a warning that you never know when you might be on Candid Camera.

Well, if you are a Christian here is news for you. You are being watched. Christians are trying to stand and walk around straight in a world where everyone else is bent and twisted from the crippling effects of sin. Christians are obvious. The very gospel they claim to believe makes them an instant target. The very light they embraced for their own salvation now emanates from them, illuminating the miserable condition of those around them.

Christians are trying to crawl out of the slime pit of the world. Those still in it are hoping that they will slip and slide back into it. They are counting on it.

You are being watched. Any person who does not know

your Lord will, rightly or wrongly, judge the validity of the claims of Christ on the basis of your life. People looking for an excuse to reject Christ are just waiting for you to give them one.

The tape is rolling in the locker room as well as in the classroom, on the playing field, on a date, and at the beach. They are hoping to see a shooting star. They are hoping to see your faith burn out. They are hoping to see you twist up and bend over again.

They are listening to every word and looking for the opportunity to say, "See, they are just like us—except they are self-righteous." There is no such thing as a candid or hidden Christian. It is in our new nature to shine. It is in our old nature to fail.

We will not disappoint those who are looking for a place of failure in our lives. But with God's help we can be guiding lights for those who wish to navigate out of their sin.

Who can you think of who might be watching your Christian life? What kind of example have you been?

Day 2 A Captive Audience

My tongue will tell of your righteous acts all day long, for those who wanted to harm me have been put to shame and confusion. Psalm 71:24

As Paul penned his letter to the church in Philippi he had constant company. It was not the cheerful companionship of a wife (Paul was evidently unmarried) nor the encouraging company of a good friend (though a few visited him often). It was the unwelcome company of an armed guard.

Paul was often in prison or under house arrest, yet he wrote with a spirit that gave little or no clue as to the confinement and physical despair of his situation.

It is simply because in the end he did not see himself as a

captive but as a free man. Like so many others who have suffered cruelly for their faith he did not view his imprisoners as his captors. Instead, he viewed them as his captives.

It does not take much imagination to think of the reactions that the various soldiers must have had when they drew the duty to stay close to this odd little man.

For some, it must have been a relief to be assigned a duty that was not hazardous. But they were chained to a most dangerous man. The love of God seeped through him. Little did they realize that they were about to embark on their most dangerous mission: to do battle with the living God—a battle they could only win by losing.

Paul undoubtedly saw that these various guards who, as free as they were to walk out the door at the end of their shift, were actually bound tight with chains of sin. Every day with them was a new opportunity to pick their locks with the Spirit of God.

The book of Acts records one incident of the conversion of Paul's captors in the town of Philippi (see Acts 16:16-40).

Sometimes it pleases God to chain us to people who desperately need the kind of loving relationship that we have with God.

Sometimes they're classmates, teammates, co-workers, parents, family members, or neighbors. Frequently they are people we would not choose to rub shoulders with. In fact, at some points we may even wish that we could escape them entirely.

But they're the ones whom God has placed in our path so that we can reflect His love to them. They are God's captive audience at the very moment they thought we were their prisoners.

Write down the names of some people to whom God has chained you. Take some time to pray for them today.

Day 3 Non-Shining Stars

> *My brothers, as believers in our glorious Lord Jesus Christ, don't show favoritism. Suppose a man comes into your meeting wearing a gold ring and fine clothes, and a poor man in shabby clothes also comes in. If you show special attention to the man wearing fine clothes and say, "Here's a good seat for you," but say to the poor man, "You stand there," or, "Sit on the floor by my feet," have you not discriminated among yourselves and become judges with evil thoughts?* James 2:1-4

Writing to Christians in the church, James brought to light a problem that was being experienced by people who were suppose to be lights themselves.

The problem was one that plagues and darkens the church even today: favoritism.

Sometimes a person who is truly shining for Jesus Christ can be very irritating to those who claim to be Christians as well. A person who is really in touch with the Creator can be abrasive to the Christian who is complacent or trying to get comfortable with the world. A real "shining star" can even be a big pain to someone who has good intentions but a bad sense of priorities. But shining stars are a particular nuisance to those who are living or thinking contrary to the teachings of Christ.

A number of years ago a small corner church in the Orange County area of Southern California began to attract large numbers of counter-culture kids. Since it was the height of the "hippie" era the majority of these people showed up at the church service dressed in the attire of the time (or the lack or it!).

The traditional members of the church were horrified by the sight of these seemingly unkempt creatures sitting in the same pews as their precious, squeaky-clean children. They panicked in revulsion.

As still larger numbers of these young people were being

magnetically drawn by God's love (manifested by the pastor and a number of the elders) some of the congregation reached their limit.

During one of the board meetings an elder stood up and voiced strong reaction to the presence of so many undesirables pouring into the church. "What is the problem with that?" asked the pastor.

The elder hemmed and hawed, having put himself in a very uncomfortable position. Finally, he replied, "Well, they are coming into the church BAREFOOTED."

"So?" replied the pastor.

"Well, they'll wreck the carpet," responded the elder lamely.

"Is that a real concern?" asked the pastor. He could see that with a few board members it might be. The pastor sunk his jaw into his hand and furrowed his brow in thought.

Late that evening he went into the church sanctuary and ripped up all of the carpet. He contacted the board members and informed them that they could now freely have the outreach continue with the flocks of young students, unhindered by the worry of messing up the carpet.

The dissenting elder left the church in a rage. The church went on to become one of the largest churches in the area with a tremendous ministry to the unsaved.

Bright lights sometimes bother those whose lights do not shine so brightly.

Do you think this pastor did the right thing? Why or why not?

Day 4 Cranking Up the Light

> *This is the verdict: Light has come into the world, but men loved darkness instead of light because their deeds were evil. Everyone who does evil hates the light, and will not come into the light for fear*

that his deeds will be exposed. But whoever lives
by the truth comes into the light, so that it may be
seen plainly that what he has done has been done
through God. John 3:19-21

One summer during my high school years I got a job helping a friend clean one of the swanky restaurants in our little
beach town. The job called for unusual hours since all of the
cleanup had to be done after the place closed. This suited us
fine because it meant that we could spend all day at the beach
and still goof around until we started work at midnight. I'm not
quite sure when we slept.

I had eaten at the restaurant only once—my usual hang-
outs were not quite so elite. But I remember the delightfully
elegant atmosphere set off by rich paneling and deep, plush
carpet. The decor was bathed in a low romantic light day and
night due to the lack of natural lighting in the architectural
design. A classy place for classy people. And first-class prices.

Rolling in at midnight, my friend and I located the restaurant stereo (first things first) and flipped from the elevator
music to the kind of scratchy rock and roll that they played in
the early morning hours. We then divided the building in half
and each worked toward the middle.

I groped along the wall until I found the control panel that
had the rheostat for the lights at my end of the building. I
cranked them up full blast. I was astonished at what I saw. In
full light the restaurant that had once looked so glamorous
looked very plain and ordinary. Much of what I had thought
was wood was really plastic or pressboard covered with contact paper. The carpet which had seemed so fresh and springy
was deeply stained with the grime of food and traffic. The
walls had smudges of food and grease. Many of the adorn-
ments now showed themselves to be cheap and tacky. Suddenly, the little beanery with the torn upholstery where I hung
out looked a lot better for the price.

What I saw was quite a bit less attractive in the full light
than it had been before I turned up the lights. It was a lot more
work to clean as well.

God has a funny way of cranking up the amount of light in our lives. It is interesting how annoyed people get when He does this—how He shows us what we are really like. Most people hate it, unless they are there for cleaning.

Write an invitation to God asking Him to put the spotlight on any sin that you might have in your life.

Day 5 A Game of Glowball

In him was life, and that life was the light of men. The light shines in the darkness, but the darkness has not understood it. John 1:4,5

The corner church had a great outreach program to junior-age kids. Every Thursday night a hundred or so kids would show up for an evening that had plenty of fun and games, but some serious Bible teaching as well.

Since most of the kids that came to the "club" were from non-Christian backgrounds there were some pretty tough customers in the lot. Since they were all boys (the girls met on another night—cooties, you know) some of them were looking for smaller kids to clobber.

To channel the energy of a group this size the "club" played some wonderfully rowdy games. One that sticks in my memory was "glowball."

Played with a phosphorescent ball about the size of a tennis ball, the object of the game was to get your team's glowball carrier from one end of the room to the other without him getting mugged. Since each team had a glowball and were trying to reach the opposite walls the players had to act both offensively and defensively. What made the game fun (and the rules impossible to enforce) was that it was played with all the lights out.

The player who carried the glowball was the target of all the other little piranha who wanted to stop him from getting to his home wall. Therefore he made it his goal to allow the little glowball to emit the least amount of its green light as possible. (It was strictly against the rules to hide the ball in an article of clothing.)

It was always a vain attempt. Anywhere that you were in that dark room you could see the glow of that green ball seeping through the fingers of its owner. You could see the light cracking through even when the poor kid was buried under six or seven kids from the opposing side. The possessor of the glowball could not hide the fact that he was carrying the prize. He was the immediate target. What he carried next to him as he crawled across the floor was too brilliant to be extinguished or hid.

In the Christian realm the light of Christ will come pouring through us if we are holding onto Him. We will be obvious in a dark world. We will be targets. The light will seep through us though we are piled up with trouble and burdens that this world throws on us. We will glow because we know Him, because we carry Him in our hearts.

Ask God to make His light glow through you today.

Day 6 When Our Light Goes Out

The Lord is my light and my salvation—whom shall I fear? The Lord is the stronghold of my life—of whom shall I be afraid? Psalm 27:1

Jennifer was thrilled. Her parents were going away for the weekend and they finally trusted her enough to let her stay home by herself. It wasn't that she was a bad kid. On the contrary. It was just that her parents were worried about leaving a girl home alone. "After all, anything could happen," they would say.

"Anything could happen if I were a boy" Jennifer would respond.

"It's not the same," she would be reminded.

"I don't know why it's not," she would reply, even though she knew what they were really trying to say and she appreciated the concern.

But this weekend it was not the same. This weekend, liberation had finally come to her house. She could prove to them that she was more than capable. She would make the house even nicer than when they left. She would even surprise them with a cake.

Jennifer busied herself creating in the kitchen, leaving, as one often does when cooking, a huge trail of unwashed dishes. She then scrounged through the cupboards and found a can of rug deodorizer. "I'll even make this old place smell fresher," she thought. She sprinkled the powder across the carpet.

Jennifer set the timer on the stove and plopped the cake inside. Then, getting the sack of birdseed from under the sink, she walked into the living room to feed her mother's finches. She had just opened the cage door when it happened. A distant pop and suddenly the entire house was plunged into darkness. Jennifer jumped back instinctively and spilled birdseed all over the couch and floor. She groped her way to the drawer where she knew her father kept a flashlight. She flicked it on and surveyed the damage. She tried every light switch in the house. None of them worked. It was obviously a power outage. She would just curl up with a book and a flashlight until the power came back on.

When she awoke the next morning, still huddled on the couch, she realized something was wrong. The power was still not on. She drove off to work and came home that evening to a dark, cold house. The home was even heated by electricity—but not tonight. Jennifer sat in the darkness, not knowing what to do and having too much pride to ask for help from friends or neighbors.

When her parents returned the next morning they were greeted by the biggest mess they had seen in a long time, and a teary-eyed Jennifer complaining that it was not her fault but that the electric company was to blame.

Her Dad simply said "Come and let me show you how to use the circuit breaker." In a few minutes the power surged through Jennifer's house. In fact, it had been there all along. It just needed to have the right switch pulled.

When the power drains from our life it is tempting to sit in our mess and wait for the juice to come back on. It is also futile. Actively seeking God is what will light us back up. Reconnecting with Him is up to us, because His power is always there.

Is God the first one you turn to when things get dark for you? Find a verse that you can have in your memory for times like that.

Week Seven
LOST AND FOUND

Day 1 One Man's Trash

> *But whatever was to my profit I now consider loss for the sake of Christ. What is more, I consider everything a loss compared to the surpassing greatness of knowing Christ Jesus my Lord, for whose sake I have lost all things. I consider them rubbish, that I may gain Christ.* Philippians 3:7,8

How would you like to have people hold you in high esteem? How would you like to be considered a "top dog" in your field? How would you like people to think that you are special, wise—a wonder kid. How would you like to have position and authority? Most people would enjoy some or all of these things. They are the things that Paul enjoyed as a religious leader of the Jews. They are the things that he gave up to get to know Christ. They are also the things that God gave back to him after awhile.

Paul did not make a deal with God to "trade" one position for another—to do great things for God if God would do great things for him. Paul simply didn't care about the world that he left behind to walk with Christ. In fact, he used very strong language to say so.

He cared no more for his old way of life than you or I would care for our tricycle when we could drive a new sports car. Paul let go or lost things that had been very important to him before.

It is not that the things he let go of were bad. They were just insignificant in comparison to the real thing of value.

Paul is not alone in this letting go or losing of things that once were so important. In Christianity it is almost commonplace for a person to let go of the very things that had once been embraced so tightly, in order to embrace Christ. If this person had been in an extremely enviable position before his or her conversion it often shocks and angers those who hear about the renunciation of the old things.

Often, the old things are not thrown away completely but are put in their proper place, far away from the controls of the heart. Either way, the melody of the person's life changes. They begin to sing God's tune.

In some ways, the Christian life is simply life on another plane. Many of the realities and necessities stay the same, such as brushing your teeth and changing the oil in the car. But the importance that those things have may be altered radically. The earthly value system is suddenly (or sometimes gradually) replaced by the heavenly one. A human being begins to think not like a human being but like an alien. Like God.

Perhaps one can get the picture by contrasting life on the Sahara with life on a lush South Sea island. Living could be done in both places. People call both places home. In fact, they are fond of both places. But one place is a far more desirable place to live.

Letting go of this world is the trademark of all who call themselves Christians. To hold onto it would be like wanting to keep the apple core when there are bowls of fresh fruit to be had.

Can you think of one thing that you let go of to be a Christian? Was it easy or hard? Why?

Day 2 The Tale of the Pearl

> *The kingdom of heaven is like treasure hidden in a field. When a man found it, he hid it again, and then in his joy went and sold all he had and bought that field.*
>
> *Again, the kingdom of heaven is like a merchant looking for fine pearls. When he found one of great value, he went away and sold everything he had and bought it.* Matthew 13:44-46

Once upon a time there was a man who sweated out a living as the collector and dealer of fine stones and pearls. He was the middleman for jewelers, miners, and divers.

His small shop was located in the port city of Caesarea, wedged between a small linen merchant and a tanner whose shop constantly emitted unpleasant odors that would creep into neighboring stores. On the rough plaster wall he had a painter carefully write: Jude bar Abram, fine jewels and pearls.

Jude's line of expertise came in the knowledge of the true value of a stone or pearl and the connection with someone anxious to buy or sell this commodity. He was used to seeing counterfeit stones and pearls and had devised his own foolproof test to determine the validity and quality of the merchandise that would be offered to him for sale.

One hot afternoon, just as Jude was preparing to close his shop, a man stepped into the doorway. He was deeply colored in face and body but his dark hair had been bleached reddish brown by constant exposure to the sun. He was dressed in the garb of a distant foreigner and spoke with an accent thick and difficult to understand. "Sir, I pray to know if you would be interested in this." On saying that he held out his hand to display the largest, most beautiful pearl Jude had ever seen.

Jude gasped with surprise and excitement. He carefully picked up the treasure and examined it. Then he coolly placed it in the man's hand and asked, "How much would you like for it?"

The stranger thought for a moment, then answered, "2,000 talents."

Jude said nothing. He knew that he could easily sell the jewel for twice that amount. But it was such a tremendous price that he was not sure that he could raise the money to buy the pearl. But there was one thing he knew for sure, that pearl could be the opening of countless doors of possibility for him, and he must have it.

Finally, he said, "Yes, I will pay that price. You will have to come back in the morning; and please show the pearl to no one."

"You have my word," said the stranger, and he shook Jude's hand to seal the agreement.

Jude raced home. He quickly ran into the house and began to drag all of his family's possessions out the door.

Jude's wife stood for a minute in shock and confusion and then began to scream, "What on earth are you doing?"

"Selling everything," said Jude between panting breaths. "Getting it all onto the roadside so that it can be purchased tonight by those traveling home."

Jude's wife started to howl in disapproval. Jude ran up to her and said, "Good woman, please trust me! I must have all of the money that I can get my hands on, but you will not be disappointed."

The poor lady gave a great sigh and sat on a nearby rock and watched her frantic husband sell off everything that they possessed.

By the end of the evening Jude had sold everything, including the family home (which they were graciously allowed to sleep in for that night).

Jude disappeared early the next morning. When he reappeared, his wife and children ran to him crying, "Father, what is it that could possibly be worth everything that we ever had?"

Jude pulled out a little leather pouch and poured out a magnificently huge pearl. "This, my dear ones. This is worth everything that we had and more, for it will give us back more than any of you can imagine."

What would be the hardest thing for you to give up or sell to follow Christ?

Day 3 A Two-Way Street

Suppose one of you has a hundred sheep and loses one of them. Does he not leave the ninety-nine in the open country and go after the lost sheep until he finds it? And when he finds it, he joyfully puts it on his shoulders and goes home. Then he calls his friends and neighbors together and says, "Rejoice with me; I have found my lost sheep." I tell you that

in the same way there is more rejoicing in heaven
over one sinner who repents than over ninety-nine
righteous persons who do not need to repent. Luke
15:4-7

Paul made a big deal out of finding Christ. He pointed out
over and over again what wonderful changes the discovery of
the Lord had made in his life.

Interestingly enough, God makes a big deal out of finding
us as well.

Not that God does not know where we were located. He
has always known that. He saw the first steps that you and I
took away from Him. He knew about the self-centered
thoughts and the prideful spirit that led us farther and farther
away from His care and guidance. He saw us tangle ourselves
in briars of sin and tear ourselves squeezing through the
barbed wire of His loving boundary lines.

And He was following us, calling to us. His shepherd's
song rang out clear and sweet many a time. We knew He was
there, but we would not come to Him. Still He tracked us
relentlessly. Watching us, waiting for us, and often compelling
us with soothing words of invitation.

But He never grabbed hold of us. It was against His nature
to force His will upon us. He simply waited for us to cry out to
Him. He waited for a word from us.

He considered no expense too great to pursue us. He gave
everything including His life to get us back to safety.

Finally, when we had come to the point where we realized
that we were about to make a total wreckage of our lives, we
called out to Him, sometimes weakly, pathetically—a thin
whimper for help.

And He was there. Swiftly, steadily picking us up and carrying us on His shoulders. Calling to heaven's inhabitants to
rejoice with Him. The one He had been pursuing for so long
was finally back at home.

Paul was right to be pleased that he found Christ. But the
reality of the situation is that Jesus was there all of the time
waiting to get Paul's undivided attention and cry for help. He

was—and is—there waiting to pick us up and carry us as well.

Take some time and write a note to yourself about times you heard Christ's voice calling you.

Day 4 A Bad Trade

> *What good will it be for a man if he gains the whole world, yet forfeits his soul?* Matthew 16:26

"Behind this door could be one of these great things: a trip around the world, a new car, or a chance to be a movie star! How 'bout it? Will you trade me what is in your hand for what is behind this door?

"The clock is ticking; you have 10 seconds left to decide . . . nine, eight, seven . . . WHAT? You will trade? Wonderful. Here is what you have won: Ohhh too bad. You won our booby prize: a pair of used sneakers. Better luck next time. Next contestant please."

Most of us are familiar with this kind of game show where a player is tempted to trade up for the chance at something bigger and better. It may make fun television but it makes for deadly reality.

We are constantly being offered something in exchange for our souls. Like the legendary Faust, who sold his soul to the devil in exchange for knowledge and power, some have entered into a conspiracy with evil. They willingly trade now for later—present gratification for future peril. Others are not as aware of the trading game or the things at stake. They are willing to entertain all offers coming their way.

We can be certain that if Satan has lost the trading game for our souls he will not give up. Instead the exchange will be offered for our righteousness. We will be asked to let go of our values and godly principles to take a risk on what is behind the door.

"Yes, just think, kid. You could be among the most popular students in your high school! All ya have to do is let go of that silly 'religious conviction' you are hanging on to and let your feelings flow. Party with us, think like us, act like us, and you've got it, kid—popularity! Whaddya say? You wanna go for it? OK. Open the doors!"

The trade is never worth it. Nothing in this world is worth trading in the ideas and values of Christ or our relationship with Him.

"Aw, kid. I'm awful sorry. You wanted popularity but I'm afraid that you've won the title of 'class clown.' I guess that will just have to do. But say, would you like to trade in that virtue you are holding onto for a hot night of cheap . . . uh, er, meaningful relationships?"

What are you being offered in exchange for your walk with Christ? Why do you think it would not be worth it to trade?

Day 5 No Baggage

> *Jesus looked at him and loved him. "One thing you lack" he said. "Go, sell everything you have and give to the poor, and you will have treasure in heaven. Then come, follow me."* Mark 10:21

"NO BAGGAGE ALLOWED" read the sign posted at the dock entrance. It was repeated a time or two again down the dock and once more just short of the gangplank. Yet still the man ahead of me had an armload of suitcases and carry-on bags.

To be polite and to save him from embarrassment, I pointed out the sign as we waited in line to board the boat. He huffed and said, "Don't you think I can read, mister?"

"Yes," I replied. I was sure that he probably could but I thought that perhaps he had overlooked the signs.

"Look, it's none of your business, but I will tell you that the captain and me have an arrangement: I will go on his ship if he will let me bring my luggage. There's things a bloke might need in here, you know."

The line moved slowly up the dock as the passengers were ushered one by one onto the small ship by ship hands dressed in blazing white uniforms.

Soon the man in front of me tried to shuffle his way onto the gangplank with his load of baggage. "I'm sorry, sir," said one of the white-clad porters cheerfully, "but the luggage must stay on shore."

"What?" roared the man. "I can't leave this luggage behind."

"Then you will not be able to board," said the porter gently and sadly.

"This is an outrage! I need my things!" yelled the man. The back of his neck, which was all I could see, was turning a crimson red. He turned to me with his face contorted by anger and eyes bulging out and exploded, "Can you believe what they are saying to me? Don't they know who I am?"

"I'm not sure that they care, sir," I said. "After all, the conditions are posted."

"They can stow their conditions!" screamed the man, now pacing the dock in complete animation of body. "I want to talk to the captain," he demanded of the porter. "He gave me permission to bring this with me."

"And when did you speak with him?" asked the porter, with a twinkle in his eye.

"I told him the other night that was how it was going to be," replied the man.

"And what did he say?" asked the porter, with a face that could not be lied to.

"Uh, well, I didn't really wait for his answer. I just assumed . . . . " the man began to say.

"You assumed incorrectly, sir," replied the porter pleasantly.

"I'm going to find another ship!" yelled the man. "One that will take me where I want to go in comfort and with my luggage."

"No other ship will take you where you really want to go," called out the porter after him. But he was gone. He was making great haste towards another ship docked in the harbor. I could just barely make out the name as the picture fogged and I began to wake up from this wild dream. It was TITANIC.

What would be your honest response if Jesus asked you to do literally what He asked the man in the Scripture passage to do?

Day 6 Why Be a Fisherman?

> As Jesus walked beside the Sea of Galilee, he saw
> Simon and his brother Andrew casting a net into
> the lake, for they were fishermen. "Come, follow
> me," Jesus said, "and I will make you fishers of
> men." At once they left their nets and followed him.
> Mark 1:16-18

Why be rich if you can give your wealth to the poor?
Why be quiet when you can bless someone with words?
Why be in discord with God when you can be in harmony?
Why stay the same when you can change?
Why watch when you can do?
Why gossip when you can pray?
Why be a fisherman when you can be a disciple?

The list is endless. Why should we satisfy ourselves with things that are second-rate or below our opportunities or potential?

Maybe we settle for half-rate things because we are not willing to put forth the effort it takes to do our best. We are a bit lazy. Perhaps it's because there is security in doing things like we always do them and we are afraid to stretch, change, or grow.

Peter was not offered a higher salary. In fact, he left his own business partnership to be indentured to a master for no pay whatsoever. He was not given a promise of position, authority, or the carefree life. He was given only the cryptic message that he could be a "fisher of men."

But he left it all behind. He put it away. He set out on a new adventure that would take him far away from the peaceful fishing village on the shore of Galilee.

Peter only returned to this occupation once after his call. He went back for a short time in the confusion that followed the Crucifixion.

There was nothing wrong with being a fisherman. It was just not the best that God had.

For each one of us God has some important things that He wants to accomplish through us. It may be important only to God and not to any other. He will do it where He meets no resistance, where He finds people who are willing to drop their plans and personal dreams in exchange for God's plan and dreams.

For some, that means the mission field, for others, A1 Car Repair Service. It is not the place but the purpose to which God still calls—to be fishers of men.

Why be a fisherman when you can be a disciple? Why be anything that is pure garbage in comparison to what God has in store?

What special things do you think God has called you to do right now? Who do they involve?

HITTING THE GOAL

Day 1 Aim at Nothing

> *Not that I have already obtained all this, or have*
> *already been made perfect, but I press on to take*
> *hold of that for which Christ Jesus took hold of me.*
> *Brothers, I do not consider myself yet to have taken*
> *hold of it. But one thing I do: Forgetting what is*
> *behind and straining toward what is ahead, I press*
> *on toward the goal to win the prize for which God*
> *has called me heavenward in Christ Jesus.*
> *All of us who are mature should take such a*
> *view of things. And if on some point you think dif-*
> *ferently, that too God will make clear to you. Only*
> *let us live up to what we have already attained.*
> Philippians 3:12-16

"Aim at nothing and you will be sure to hit it," a wise friend told me long ago. I've thought about that a lot and have come to see how true it is.

Life seems to be divided into two types of people. Those who try to float through life and those who paddle through it.

The floaters have no distinct goal. They move within the currents that swirl around them, but they rarely paddle against them. They will often reach out for a goal that is within their grasp but will seldom run the risk of setting out for any objective that requires great effort.

The paddlers, on the other hand, often move against the common current. They generally have a distinct objective that they are trying to reach and will pursue this objective whether anyone joins them or not.

Naturally, some personality types are more inclined to be paddlers and some are more inclined to be floaters, but there is one place where floating through life is not allowed. That is in Christianity. Christians are, or should be, people who have a goal. The goal is to become perfect. The model for this perfection is Christ Himself.

You cannot float through life and become like Christ. It takes effort. It takes small, concentrated steps. It takes knowing where you are going. Christianity requires those who are floaters by nature to work on changing that nature. It requires those who are paddlers by nature to change the goal that they paddle for. It is a very common sin for "paddler"-type people to chase after something good, even religious, rather than after becoming like Christ.

To paddle after the wrong goal means that we can end up sitting on a barren rock of existence that was not worth the effort to find.

To float with the current of culture is to eventually be dashed and wasted upon the rocks of despair. To paddle for something that won't satisfy is bad; to float after something that never satisfies is worse.

The Christian experience is one of taking constant aim, watching the One we are following. We will miss our target many times. We will often fall short of the mark. But we will know what it is that we are aiming our lives toward.

What is the goal of your life?

Day 2 Strip and Swim

> *Therefore, since we are surrounded by such a great cloud of witnesses, let us throw off everything that hinders and the sin that so easily entangles, and let us run with perseverance the race marked out for us.* Hebrews 12:1

Every summer, beaches all around the nation are crowded with people hoping to escape the inland heat by migrating to the more temperate seaside.

Generally, the beach areas cooperate with summer and produce warm sand and water temperature that is enjoyable for swimming. Occasionally the ocean refuses to cooperate and, instead of warmth, sends a chilly current of ice water in tandem with a beautiful, warm day.

As a year-round beach resident, I find it interesting and often humorous to watch the reactions of those who plunge into the sea expecting it to be as warm as the hotel swimming pool, only to find that they are quickly becoming human popsicles.

Some, of course, seem to have no end of determination to enjoy the cold water ("After all, Martha, we came 300 miles to go for a swim and by cracky that's what I'm gonna do!").

Every year there is a handful of people during those chilly water weeks who decide to swim and stay warm at the same time. In a very unusual way, they wear a T-shirt.

Now there are ways to stay comfortable in cold water. A wetsuit is the best way. But wearing a regular cotton T-shirt for warmth just doesn't cut it.

One of the main things that a T-shirt or heavy article of clothing will do for you in the water is slow you down, causing you to get colder faster. Clothing in the water also gets in the way of decent swimming as well as making one look rather dippy.

All of this may seem like a very silly lack of common sense to you but the way that many Christians conduct their lives is very similar to swimming in the cold ocean with a shirt on for warmth.

Many will add excess baggage in their attempt to live and think like a Christian—baggage that has no place in the Christian life. Some do this out of a false sense of security in the same way that those who wear a T-shirt in the water think that it will keep them warm. They want to have Christianity and something else—their money, their own way of thinking, or something else. Some will carry with them relationships that they shouldn't have or grudges and bitter feelings that they shouldn't hold on to; others will try to make the journey burdened down with various material possessions. What God really wants us to do is to strip and swim.

Can you think of anything that holds you back from living the Christian life the way you would want to?

Day 3 Running for Freedom

> *Do you not know that in a race all the runners run,*
> *but only one gets the prize? Run in such a way as*
> *to get the prize.* 1 Corinthians 9:24

Gaius was a slave. He had been sold into slavery at the age of 11 along with his brothers and sisters. It was his parents' "reward" for being involved in an insurrection against a certain Roman ruler of their district. His father saw his family sold into slavery and was then crucified with the other members of the insurrection. His mother committed suicide a year or so later.

Gaius had little that would endear him to any master. He was tall and gangly. His curly hair and bronzed complexion betrayed African heritage. He was illiterate and virtually unskilled. But there was one thing that Gaius could do. He could run.

Such endurance and speed did Gaius display that he soon found himself the official messenger for his master and his master's friends. If it needed to get there quickly they called Gaius to the task.

In those days, you could count on being a slave forever unless you found special favor with your master or could somehow win your freedom.

The colosseum was filled with desperate men willing to risk their lives in battle with other slaves in order to win the prize that was far above the wreath given to the winners. The prize was freedom. With victory came freedom. The master, rich from the winnings of his slave, was obligated to set the slave free as a reward.

But that kind of battle was beyond the skill of Gaius. There was one thing in which he could compete that he felt certain he had a chance to win—a race.

It took little time to convince his master that he could increase his wealth considerably by entering his slave in various footraces. Gaius won them with ease. But the larger the cities in which he raced, the stiffer the competition. Until the day he came to race in Rome.

This was the pinnacle of the footrace. The finest runners were all here. They were all slaves and they all had their eyes fixed on one goal. Freedom.

At the signal, Gaius sprang forward, the competition surging around him. He did not see them; all he could picture was himself as a free man. His mind filled with images of walking the streets at his own will, of having his own family that could not be separated from him, of serving whom he wanted or not serving anyone at all. The lure of liberty made him fly like he had never done before. When he crossed the finish line, chest heaving, crowds cheering, he knew he had laid hold of the best prize he could win.

In our Christian life the ultimate goal is freedom. Freedom from a sin nature that drags on us like weights; freedom from the suffering and sorrow of this world; freedom to be the kind of people that God is changing us into at last. It is a goal well worth the reach. And we can reach it.

Describe what kind of prize you think is in store for a Christian who successfully runs the race.

Day 4 Toughen Up

Therefore I do not run like a man running aimlessly; I do not fight like a man beating the air. No, I beat my body and make it my slave so that after I have preached to others, I myself will not be disqualified for the prize. 1 Corinthians 9:26,27

Every year after a long summer vacation Tom and I would find that we had once again ended up in the same PE class.

During that long summer Tom and I had not shot one basket, thrown one football, jogged one mile, or done one sit-up. We surfed instead. Board surfed, body surfed, boogie-board surfed, swam, dived, and floated. That was why the first day together in gym class was such a killer. Our bodies were in great shape for the water but in lousy shape for land.

The first thing that we were required to do was to run a mile around the track. Tom and I would set off at a confident pace—almost a sprint—sure that our summer of hard play had tuned us to be universally fit. Wrong! By the second lap the complaint of muscles not used for three months began to be felt. By the third, the lungs seemed to be screaming for relief. Still the coach would not let anyone quit or walk and get by with a halfway passing grade. By the fourth lap all the guys who were runners, joggers, or even skippers sailed by us as we dragged ourselves around the track.

The last couple of laps were pure torture. The pain had gone up the lungs and into the air pipe. The inside of my mouth was dry; breath came hard. Tom wasn't doing much better. His eyes were at half-mast and his tongue was hanging out of his mouth. We staggered past the coach on our last lap and collapsed in the grass. "Well, it looks like school's started," said Tom when he finally got a breath.

"Yeah," I gasped. "Some fun, huh?"

We lay on the lawn and paid a price for being out of shape for the run. In fact, we paid it the first week of every year of high school.

It is one thing to be out of shape for a run around the track. It is entirely another thing to be out of shape to run the race of life. Winning that game takes discipline, both mental and physical—giving ourselves duties and goals that will require effort, running until our heavenly Coach says that we can stop to rest.

Few Christians today experiment with the kind of tough self-discipline described by Paul. We pamper ourselves, not drive ourselves. We make excuses for ourselves rather than get tough with ourselves. We compare ourselves to the other softies around us rather than trying to stay in "running shape." We wait until we are forced into a situation to get in condition rather than being in good condition in case we end up in a situation where endurance is needed.

Getting tough with ourselves means that we deny ourselves. It means that we push ourselves to limits that we didn't think we could make. When we do we may find to our surprise and delight that we could do a lot more than we thought— and not even be winded.

Make a list of the things that you deny yourself or discipline yourself to do because you are a Christian. What would you add to this list to push you a lap further in the Christian life?

Day 5 The Way Home

> *I will instruct you and teach you in the way you*
> *should go; I will counsel you and watch over you.*
> Psalm 32:8

Ron gets his kicks out of visiting out-of-the-way places. *Way* out-of-the-way places. Places that few westerners have ever seen. Remote jungle areas of South America or New Guinea.

In these dense jungles one must live and eat with the native inhabitants whose diet consists of strange things like grubs and once-chewed banana beverages. Some tribes are so fascinated by the visitor that the whole crowd shows up to watch Ron go to the bathroom (second tree to the right) or clean up in the river. They poke at him while he sleeps and play with his light-colored hair.

These people are not civilized in our sense of the word but that doesn't mean they are stupid. They know how to get around in their neighborhood, and they think it odd that we can't figure our way out of the bush once we get in it.

For the residents of that area the jungle is as distinctive as is each block and the houses on it in our neighborhood. They can find their way home through the thick mass of tangled vegetation as easily as we can take short cuts through a vacant lot or down the alleyway.

During one visit to these fascinating people Ron was the victim of one of their practical jokes.

While hiking down the remote and rugged jungle trail with a large group of his native friends, Ron suddenly looked up to find that the entire group had vanished into the jungle—without a trace.

He called out their names and was met with only silence. He tried to find his way back to the camp but found that the trail had disappeared into the thick bush. For hours he tried to find his way out of the undergrowth until he gave up hope and sat down on the jungle floor, exhausted and in despair.

Suddenly the whole group came laughing out of the bush. They had been with him the whole time and had followed his every move. He was never lost (at least, not in their minds). He had never seen them. They had the time of *his* life as a great practical joke.

God knows the way through the territory in which we get quite lost. It is His home ground. He will guide us and lead us. And best of all, He will never disappear and leave us helpless—not even as a joke.

How do you think God guides you? Give some examples.

Day 6 Being There

Therefore, my dear brothers, stand firm. Let nothing move you. Always give yourselves fully to the work of the Lord, because you know that your labor in the Lord is not in vain. 1 Corinthians 15:58

Does it ever seem like most of the fun of a trip is the preparation and anticipation that one goes through before actually getting there?

First there is the fun of imagining where in the world to go. A South Sea island; the Alps; dark, hidden jungles; a huge cultural city; or back to the farm? So many choices in a big world.

Then come the travel brochures and the squeezing of information from people who have been there.

Finally, the arrangement of schedules, airline tickets, and the selection of clothing to pack. By this time the excitement can be incredible. The trip to the airport can make you a nervous wreck and when that big baby takes off into the blue sky it can seem like the highlight of the trip. It often is. Many times being there is not as exciting as getting ready to go there. (It usually comes in a close second if you are going to someplace nice, though.)

The Christian life is one of getting "there." But so many people have so vague an idea of where "there" is that after awhile it seems that the constant effort to be a Christian in word and deed is all in vain. We have a fuzzy idea of where we are supposedly heading but the progress is slow and difficult at times.

"There" for a Christian is a number of things. First of all, it is to be face-to-face with God. This is difficult to imagine. There are no travel flyers that can adequately display what this will be like. The best that we can imagine will be but a flicker of the vast amounts of love, warmth, comfort, acceptance, joy, and delight that awaits those who are part of God's family.

"There" is also a place—a new heaven and earth. A recreation in some grand design that is really known only to the Architect. It will rival the most majestic creation of this world at every turn.

"There" is also a way that we will find ourselves. We will be made complete. We will be new, fulfilled, purified. We will be finally rid of the things that plagued and pestered us all of our lives. We will look in the mirror and find that we have new timeless and ageless bodies and we will see that our character has become like that of our Master.

Being "there" will be anything but a letdown, because "there" is not a place that you visit and then go home. It is home itself. It is one case where the preparation and effort are never in vain. It is one place from which you will never want to return.

Do you ever get discouraged, putting so much effort into the Christian life? If so, write a short reminder of what your goal is and put it somewhere that you will see it next time you get tired of trying.

Week Nine

NO OTHER GODS

Day 1 Enemies of the Cross

Join with others in following my example, brothers, and take note of those who live according to the pattern we gave you. For, as I have often told you before and now say again even with tears, many live as enemies of the cross of Christ. Their destiny is destruction, their god is their stomach, and their glory is in their shame. Their mind is on earthly things. But our citizenship is in heaven. And we eagerly await a Savior from there, the Lord Jesus Christ, who, by the power that enables him to bring everything under his control, will transform our lowly bodies so that they will be like his glorious body. Philippians 3:17-21

It is hard to find people who will say bad things about God. They may make jokes that mention Him but usually the jokes are not about Him. Most people don't want to make Him their enemy—even if they are not sure that He exists. They don't want to take chances.

It is equally difficult to find people who will say bad things about Christ. They often tip their hat to Him as a good and noble teacher and then proceed to drill Christians as narrow-minded for believing the very things that Christ taught.

I have yet to hear a person bad-mouth the Holy Spirit. Some are even aware of some kind of curse if you invoke His name. He is usually just not talked about at all or He is given some giant mystical description like the "force."

It seems that no one is really bucking to make him or her-self a direct enemy of God. (You may find an odd one here or there who rants at God but there are relatively few.) Yet God has plenty of enemies.

The teaching of the Scripture is very clear on this point. A person is on one side or the other. There is no neutral ground. Hot or cold, for or against, in or out, gathering or scattering—this is the language of God. Uncomfortable language.

God will stand for no substitutes. He will allow nothing to

take His place as the Lord in a person's life. The minute people erect their own deities they become enemies of the cross of Christ.

They have chosen sides. They have crossed the line that will lead them into an ever-downward spiral of inner decay and destruction. The process is sadly subtle. God is rarely replaced in the life of a Christian in one fell swoop. He is generally nudged out of the way. He becomes less and less important, many times being replaced by good things or necessities of life, until one day He is no longer God.

Obviously, there can be no real substitutes for God. They will fade in comparison to Him. They will have to be replaced over and over again while He is timeless. They will be empty and unsatisfying while He will be filling and quenching. Yet many—most, in fact—invest in erecting those things that cannot possibly last in the chamber of the King of Kings and then bow down and worship it. In doing so they become enemies of the One who came to this planet to be their most true and trusted friend.

On a piece of paper make a list, in the order of priority, of the things that are the most important in your life. Where is God? Is your life really lived by your list?

Day 2 The Shiny Idol

Dear children, keep yourselves from idols. 1 John 5:21

Roger always took good care of his idol. Each Saturday morning he would go to the little side room that had been built just to house it, and would carefully pull the covering off of it. There his idol stood, bright, golden metal of incredible size and weight. This idol was not some cheap Tiki god that he could wear around his neck.

Roger moved the idol into the outdoor sunlight and prepared for the now-established ritual. Taking the idol outdoors would not only facilitate its cleaning but would allow all of those who passed by to gaze in awe and reverence at his god. Roger gently bathed the idol to remove any of the dust particles that might diminish its shine and then smeared the idol with a sweet scented lotion like an offering to his god. He then wiped off the idol with a deerskin rag, causing it to glow and reflect beams of light in every direction.

Roger then took great pains to polish to a high gloss the plate that stated the idol's name.

Many others maintained their idols on the same day and in similar fashion. You could see them as you strode through the city streets, waxing, polishing, and worshiping.

There were some who were careless with their idols. They were held in great disdain by Roger and his friends. "It's obvious that they don't know what is important," Roger would comment in his more generous moments.

By and large, much of Roger's time and energy was spent in service to His god. He would talk and brag to his friends about the tremendous power and abilities of his idol. They would then counter back with stories of their idols' omnipotence.

Occasionally the others would bring over their idols and they would compare capabilities of each of the gods they served.

Sometimes others would come and stare at the idol Roger owned. This made him especially proud. His god did strike an impressive figure and the attention the god received was much of the reason that Roger served it as he did.

When Roger would get finished with his Saturday of cleaning and polishing his idol, he would stand back and think of what a fine thing it was, and then get in, start it up, and drive it downtown.

Can you make a list of idols that people you know serve?

Day 3 The Gumby God

You shall have no other gods before me. Exodus
20:3

One of the corniest creatures to ever hit the TV screen has
got to be Gumby and his pal Pokey. Gumby is so corny that he
even has sort of a cult following among certain high school
and college campuses.

Gumby is a clay man—er, uh, a clay thing. Pokey is his
horse. He is able to be molded into any shape that is conven-
ient for the story line of the film. He can bend completely
backward, roll in a ball, or flatten out like a pancake. He is pliable, moldable, and very hard to take even the slightest bit seriously.

There is a god around who is very much like Gumby. This
god is also very pliable. He molds to the wishes of his creator.
He obeys commands. He hides his eyes when there is something that he is not to see; he will bend over backwards to not
offend his master or to make a wrong situation right. Or he will
at least offer a reasonable exception for the individuals
involved so they will not have to deal with guilt.

The Gumby god is a very popular god. People love him.
They often pay homage to him right alongside someone else
who is worshiping a completely different God.

But the Gumby god is much more fun. If there is some
action that the owner needs, some justification for wrong
actions, he can just pray and (with a little help) the Gumby
god will nod his rubbery head in approval. The Gumby god is
portable and can be taken along on any journey through life.
He is also small enough to be stuffed in the pocket so as to be
out of sight most of the time, only to be called on in case of
emergencies. The Gumby god is great for quick blessings or
sanctifying just about anything.

The Gumby god has a great deal to his credit. He gave the
go-ahead to launch the crusades as well as the salve to calm
the consciences of Nazi supporters during World War II. He
has given countless people the right to steal, cheat, become
immoral—because they were exceptions to the rules. Gumby

god said so. But, of course, with the Gumby god, one is always the exception to the rules.

Most people recognize that the Gumby god is powerless. But that is the way that he is desired to be. If he had any power he might try to use it to take control and become like the God that other people serve. The Gumby god is loved for the precise reason that he is not demanding. He is not God for the same reason.

Take a moment to prayerfully examine your own heart to see if you are trying to manipulate God in any way.

Day 4 Can They Give Rain?

> *Do any of the worthless idols of the nations bring rain? Do the skies themselves send down showers? No, it is you, O Lord our God. Therefore our hope is in you, for you are the one who does all this.* Jeremiah 14:22

In the vast expanses of deserts that cover the United States, a traveler can often witness a phenomenon known as a mirage. Across the blistering black pavement of long, stretched-out highways, there often appears a shimmer which looks deceptively like water. It is a false promise. For the closer one gets to the mirage the farther down the highway it becomes. It can only be chased. It can never be captured.

Even in our modern world there are many false gods that promise the refreshment of inner peace and tranquility when all that they really provide is a distant view of what could be.

From the way some people talk, one would think that true happiness could come tumbling down from any variety of sources. From romance novels one gets the idea that the perfect man (or woman) will bring that "happily ever after" promised in the storybooks. From popular records and video one gets the idea that attaining stardom and popularity will cause the path to become golden. Others reach out to take from the elusive pot of gold at the end of the rainbow of business to bring them the satisfaction that they are seeking. Some seek to drench themselves in a constant flow of fast living and thrills to fill the void inside.

There is one problem with all of the other gods that people in our society serve: they can't do what they are supposed to do.

The One who is the true source of rain, sun, and wind is also the very same One who is the true source of peace, joy, and happiness. He has many contenders but no competition. They are cheap imitations, painted up and portrayed as things to be sought after and even worshiped. But they are powerless to give what they claim.

False gods may shine in the sun but they do not create the sunshine; they may accept our labor and love but they cannot return it; they may ask us to die for them but they are incapable of dying for us. False gods often have the appearance of deity. They seem majestic, powerful, compelling, and often authoritative. Some are still disguised as religions or philosophies; others have taken the disguise of twentieth-century idols. But like their ancient predecessors they may be able to sit in the rain, describe the rain, or even tell why and when it will rain. They cannot create the rain.

The final test of any modern-day gods is whether or not they can really perform. They cannot. The first results may look promising but in the final analysis there is nothing but failure.

Why, then, do people seek after them? Some know of no better way. They have never comprehended the real God and worship substitutes out of ignorance. Others are seeking a quick and painless solution from a deity that is not demanding.

Others really do believe that their god can "give the rain." They have believed the false publicity and figure they can find satisfaction for the deep and incredible thirst that they have inside them.

Ignorance, laziness, or sincere but vain beliefs may offer

many things but there is only One who speaks the Word and fills the dryness of the soul with His living water, just as He cools the parched land with His rain.

List as many false claims as you can think of that modern-day gods make. What are some of the claims that our true God makes?

Day 5 Don't Look Back

> So you are no longer a slave, but a son; and since you are a son, God has made you also an heir.
> Formerly, when you did not know God, you were slaves to those who by nature are not gods. But now that you know God—or rather are known by God—how is it that you are turning back to those weak and miserable principles? Do you wish to be enslaved by them all over again? Galatians 4:7-9

A person's memory is a very funny thing. By our very nature most of us will try to forget the negative things and remember the positive things.

For example, in the maternity ward of any hospital one can hear women in labor saying some pretty mean things about their husbands. You can ask them how they feel about having more children and if you didn't get cussed out you would almost certainly get a "you've-got-to-be-kidding"-type of answer from a large majority.

The funny thing is that the very same women who swore that they would never let their husbands within 20 feet of them again are, a few months later, "thinking about having another baby" and a few years later have forgotten all the pain and are pregnant again.

This tendency to forget pain really helps for things like having babies or going to the dentist. But it is really dangerous when it moves into other areas.

For those of us who got a full mouthful of the world before we became Christians, the tendency can be to forget the emptiness and bitterness of a life in opposition to Christ and to remember only the fun bits. In fact, we will often amplify the good parts to be better than they really were.

The Bible demonstrates that this is not unique to twentieth-century people. Lot's wife turned in longing to look back at Sodom and never went any further down the road. The children of Israel marching around the wilderness started to long for the good things that they remembered about Egypt, forgetting the cruel slavery that they had been rescued from.

It is easy to forget that we were once slaves to things that didn't matter and never will. It is easy to forget that we once worshiped gods that were phony and worthless, and that we worshiped them with great passion.

The tragedy is that some Christians, even some of you reading these words, will go back to slavery. Of course, at the time they will not see it as slavery but as some sort of liberation from silly ideas, or they will see themselves as the great exclusion from keeping God's rules. Generally, they find themselves in a deeper mess than God originally pulled them out of.

The little voice will always be there. "It wasn't so bad in Egypt; think of all the good times you had," it will whisper. It will not speak of the pain. Only a fool will heed it; only a fool looks back.

Write yourself a note reminding you of what the world really has to offer in comparison to following Christ.

Day 6 Arms Outstretched

> *Will you steal and murder, commit adultery and perjury, burn incense to Baal and follow other gods you have not known, and then come and stand*

*before me in this house, which bears my Name,
and say, "We are safe"—safe to do all these detest-
able things?* Jeremiah 7:9,10

Any student of the Bible has run across the god Baal in the pages of Scripture. Baal was an idol of the Phoenicians who generally was considered the god of nature. During the time when the judges ruled Israel, Baal was often worshiped by the Hebrew people, sometimes right alongside the true God.

This may seem rather odd until one realizes that most of the people of Israel mingled and even intermarried with Baal worshipers. There was quite a bit of social pressure to join the company of the idol worshipers. It was the trendy things to do.

Idols representing Baal have been found in various sizes and postures, perhaps the most insidious of which has been the statue of the god with arms outstretched.

It was this same pose that was created for use in the human sacrifice to the god Baal. Bigger-than-life statues of the god were created out of metal. The idol was then brought before the people and heated until the arms glowed red hot. The frenzied mass of worshipers were then asked to sacrifice something dear to them to the god Baal. They brought forward their own children and had them burned alive in the fiery outstretched arms of Baal.

As horrifying as we might think this action was, it is still in practice today. Not in the same exact fashion—not in the arms of a red-hot idol—but similar in evilness and personal destruction.

Baal's arms are still outstretched. Baal is no longer called by that name but is now called by countless others. He still asks for sacrifices. He asks for our integrity, our purity, our faith. He calls for our time, our industry, our talent. If he gets those, he will ask for more. Some will eventually give him their friends, family, and even their own children. In his arms all of those good things will be destroyed.

Some will try to worship two gods, one which is true and the other which is false. Both are demanding. The word that came to Jeremiah speaks of God's indignation when this is attempted.

The false gods are calling us. Their arms are outstretched. Their promoters promise the world to those who will crawl up onto their limbs. But there stands another with His arms outstretched as well. He has nailprints in His hands from the time He was a sacrifice—the only one that would have to be made. Now the arms are outstretched, not to take from us but to hold us.

Read the verse above again. Is there anything that you need to confess to God or ask forgiveness for before you try to serve Him?

Can you think of anything that you would have to sacrifice to serve a false god?

Week Ten
REJOICE

Day 1 Keep in Touch

> *Rejoice in the Lord always. I will say it again:*
> *Rejoice! Let your gentleness be evident to all. The*
> *Lord is near. Do not be anxious about anything, but*
> *in everything, by prayer and petition, with thanks-*
> *giving, present your requests to God. And the peace*
> *of God, which transcends all understanding, will*
> *guard your hearts and your minds in Christ Jesus.*
> Philippians 4:4-7

Do you remember the first major crush that you had on another person? How about the first major crush that was mutual? Whew! Talk about intensity. You probably hung out at his or her locker. You probably placed yourself in areas where you would be sure to cross paths (even if it was far out of your way). Every chance you had, you were there. Even during the times that you couldn't physically be together you probably talked to each other on the phone. You probably talked about just about everything that you could think of and when you ran out of things to talk about you probably just listened to each other breathe over the line.

Very possibly this great crush ended in a rather short time span and as you are reminded of some of the silly things that you did it may very well embarrass you or make you think what a creep that person turned out to be.

The point is that you keep in touch with those in whom you're interested. You talk to them—you tell them things that you wouldn't tell just anyone.

God wants you to keep in touch with Him as well. Of course, you will want to do that if you really care about Him. The truth is that many times the reason we don't keep in touch with Him is that, regardless of what we say, we don't care enough about Him. But what are we to say to Him? Doesn't it seem kind of like a one-way conversation?

God wants us to tell Him what is in our heads and on our hearts. He wants to hear our anger, our thanks, and our joy. He wants to hear our wants and desires. He wants to hear our frustrations, sadness, and disappointment as well as the things that we are excited about. He wants to hear about the mundane little things that NOBODY else would think were worth hearing about as well as the heavy crisis stuff.

God wants to answer us as well. His answers can be yes, no, maybe, wait, go, stop, rest, learn, as well as a number of others. He wants to give us our heart's desire but at the same time He wants to change our hearts.

But if we are to rejoice, pray, petition, or complain, we have to stay in touch, even if it just means hearing the Holy Spirit breathing in our lives and sighing back ourselves. If it has been a long time since you really talked with God, keep in touch.

Make a list of things in the categories mentioned above that you would like to talk to God about.

Day 2 Make a Joyful Noise

> *Shout for joy to the Lord, all the earth. Serve the Lord with gladness; come before him with joyful songs. Know that the Lord is God. It is he who made us, and we are his; we are his people, the sheep of his pasture.*
> *Enter his gates with thanksgiving and his courts with praise; give thanks to him and praise his name. For the Lord is good and his love endures forever; his faithfulness continues through all generations.* Psalm 100

The Wednesday night youth meeting was about to begin. We shuffled to the hall that was completely bare except for a line of chairs around the perimeter of the walls, a scattering of Bibles on the floor, and a stool and microphone in the front of the room. For some unknown reason this meeting had really taken off. We suspected that it was God at work. It had been doubling almost every month in size and was now literally bursting out of the hall, the biggest room in the church. Kids from every social level in the school had shown up there. They had heard that something good was happening, and they were right. But it was not always what they expected.

One of the young leaders got up and began leading the group in a round of simple choruses that helped focus attention upward as well as giving a good clue to any newcomer that all these kids were here to learn about God.

It was during that first song that I heard it. Weaving in and out through the solid wall of uplifted voices came a weird sound. I strained to hear it better but the noise ended as soon as the chorus did. "Maybe some sort of feedback from the mike," I thought. Our PA equipment was always doing weird things like picking up some ultra-high-powered Mexican radio station and broadcasting it in the background.

During the next song I heard the odd sound again. It was almost a gurgling—certainly not an electronic noise; it was almost animal. "Perhaps it is one of the neighbors' dogs howling at our singing," I mused. The thought opened the door to some funny mental pictures. Old Rover next door trying to howl out "Amazing Grace." Instantly my mind filled with great absurdities. New hit album: "The Gospel Poodles Sing." "I Bark for Jesus." "Fido Sings the Best of Amy Grant." Another blast of the bizarre sound popped my mind back to reality.

Curiosity overwhelmed me and I slipped out the side door to investigate. The sound was more distinct and coming from the direction of the double doors that opened to the center of the hall. There was a knot of people spilling outside the room. In fact, there were people sitting in the open windows. All of them were singing loudly, but the sound seemed to be coming from the center of the group at the door's edge. I wedged myself into the tight cluster of people and saw a young man in a wheelchair, his body cocked in various angles, bent with the crippling disease cerebral palsy—a condition which deforms the body but leaves the mind sharp and intact. He was singing at the top of his lungs to his God. He wasn't really singing, he was making noise—a strange, distorted, off-key sound being produced by a body that wouldn't obey the mind. But it was a joyful noise. I recall walking away thinking that it was undoubtedly the sweetest and most joyful noise that God had heard all evening.

Try creating your own song to sing exclusively to God.

Day 3 Overflowing Joy

> *He put a new song in my mouth, a hymn of praise to our God. Many will see and fear and put their trust in the Lord.* Psalm 40:3

The sun came streaking through the cracks in the clouds, creating spotlights of golden color on the side of the building and up the grassy hills. The street and cars, still wet from the night's rain, picked up every escaping beam and ricocheted it from one droplet to another, producing diamond-shaped flashes of condensed white light.

The morning was crisp, sweater weather—the kind that makes you alert but not cold. It was still quiet as I walked to school, and the smell of freshness had not yet been chased away by the stench of diesel and auto fumes.

The whole scene seemed to suggest the majesty, beauty, care, power, and wisdom of the Creator.

Oddly, a song came to mind—an old hymn that I had heard as a kid but seldom sang in youth groups today. The words went: "Holy, Holy, Holy! Lord God Almighty! Early in the morning our song shall rise to Thee."[1] The words and melody came flooding back on that six-block walk to school.

It was not like one of those silly songs or jingles that get stuck in your head all day that you wish you could get rid of. It was a melody that unveiled itself during a time of reflection on God's creation. It was the kind of song that you would want to stay.

I began to sing the song over and over to myself. Soon, all of the verses came back.

I cocked my head back and drank in the glory of the disintegrating storm and the overtaking sunrise. That song, "Holy, Holy, Holy," rang in my heart and mind. Without my realizing it, the words began to form on my lips and to quietly be whispered, then sung.

Hands in pockets, I strolled down the alley shortcut to school singing "Holy, Holy, Holy! Lord God Almighty! Early in the morning our song shall rise to Thee; Holy, Holy, Holy! Merciful and mighty! God in three Persons, blessed Trinity."

Suddenly I was jerked back into another world. You'll notice that I didn't say "reality." I'm not so sure that what was going on wasn't much more real than what we usually pass off as reality. I was on the school grounds and a friend was asking, "What in the world are you singing?"

I stood with the sort of look on my face that spelled puzzlement to everyone around, but it was really contemplation. "Uh, um, just a little song I know," I said, not out of embarrassment but because it didn't seem the kind of experience my friend would understand or appreciate—sort of casting of pearls before swine. It was a private bit of rejoicing that needed to stay that way.

What are some of the things that cause you to praise God?

Footnote
1. Reginald Heber, "Holy, Holy, Holy." First published in 1826.

Day 4 The Hummer

Speak to one another with psalms, hymns and spiritual songs. Sing and make music in your heart to the Lord. Ephesians 5:19

Once there was an old man who traveled through life

humming, whistling, and singing a certain melody. The tune was infectious. It was found that others who came near him or worked with him often went away humming the same melody as well, or they at least had the tune ringing in their heads.

In fact, almost anything the man did seemed to blend into the song or somehow seemed to become a part of the song. When he painted, the strokes of the brush seemed to flow in harmony with the song he hummed. If he repaired shoes, every tap of the hammer suggested the beat of his song. Even when he toiled in the field the long stems of wheat seemed to sway with the notes that he sang. There was simply no part of his life that did not in some strange way join in the song.

Sometimes the song became a dance, catchy and upbeat, lifting to their feet all those around in celebration. Other times the song was soft and thoughtful, even bittersweet, bringing a strange mix of peace even in times of tremendous sadness.

Sometimes other voices would try to drown out the melody. Their shouts and wails could not hide that clear rhythm of his song.

One day a group of men decided that they would silence the hummer. His song was not pleasant to them but was a powerful reminder of the stark silence in their own lives.

They put the old man in a lonely cell. They removed from him everyone he loved. But in the darkness of the cell his song filled the small room and seeped out the cracks in the door and flooded the dark prison with sweetness. When his enemies realized what was happening they became infuriated and had the minstrel put to death. But even as the guards were carrying away the old man's lifeless body the song he sang could be heard being gently hummed from cell after cell of that cold and hostile prison. Soon the melody was raised by voices singing in various harmonies and pitches and all of those present thought very privately that they could hear the old man humming strongly and confidently above all the others.

If your life were a song what would be the theme?

Day 5 The Laughing Place

> *Who, then, is the man that fears the Lord? He will*
> *instruct him in the way chosen for him. He will*
> *spend his days in prosperity, and his descendants*
> *will inherit the land. The Lord confides in those*
> *who fear him; he makes his covenant known to*
> *them.* Psalm 25:12-14

One of my favorite stories as a kid was the Br'er Rabbit tale from the Laughing Place.

For those of you who don't remember, the rabbit is the constant target of Br'er Fox and Br'er Bear. Occasionally the rabbit gets caught by these two bullies who are determined to make a meal of him. In all cases the quick-thinking rabbit out-smarts the greedy duo.

In the tale of the Laughing Place, the rabbit gets caught in a snare by the fox and bear. Seeing the predicament that he is in, the rabbit begins to laugh uncontrollably. He even screams with laughter as the fox and bear try to terrify him with grue-some descriptions of what they are going to do with him before they skin him alive and cook him. His amusement in the face of torture baffles and irritates the two captors, who are being robbed of the joy they had hoped to have watching the little rabbit sweat.

Finally the pair demand to know why the rabbit is laughing in the face of sure and horrible death. The cunning rabbit just giggles, "I'm just thinking of my laughing place."

In the typical, greedy fashion of some people, the fox and bear cannot stand to have anyone enjoy something unless they can have it too. So they force the rabbit to show them his laughing place before they skin him alive.

The rabbit pretends to reluctantly show them the spot and then laughs all the way to an old tree with a huge hole in its trunk. "In there," points the rabbit. The two villains fight each other to be the first to thrust their heads into the opening of the tree trunk. When they do they are met with a swarm of angry bees who have made a hive in the hole. The rabbit laughs hysterically as the fox and bear go yelping into the sunset. "That's why I call it MY laughing place," says the rabbit, as he rolls on the ground with laughter.

In a similar way, Christians can have their laughing place with God. It may be a thought or passage that is for them only—a place in God's Word that chases away the evil and temptations that try to snare us. Maybe a thought or passage that just makes one smile with joy, rest, or peace.

It can be a verse of Scripture, a line from a song, a poem or proverb, a quote from a sage. Whatever it is, it can be great fun to have your own laughing place with God.

Jot down a note reminding yourself of your secret laughing place. If you don't have one take the time to look one up in the Bible.

Day 6 Thanks for Nothing

Be joyful always. 1 Thessalonians 5:16

My pet goldfish was found floating upside down this morning. Praise God! The engine in my car just threw a rod. Hallelujah! I'm going to flunk math for the fifth time. Give God the glory!

Sound silly? You bet! Yet there are people who have a particular idea that the Bible suggests we are to thank God FOR all the things that happen to us, regardless of whether they are good or bad. Some people even use certain verses to back up this idea. Of course, you can use selected verses to back up just about anything that you wish to build a case for.

Bad things often happen to people who love God very much. Sometimes not just bad things but terrible things. God never intended for us to be happy about those things nor to thank Him for allowing them to happen to us. For example: one would not thank God for allowing a plane that you are flying in to crash killing everyone aboard except you, although you might thank Him that you made it out alive.

It is true that bad things can cause growth and insight that one could never get any other way, but it is highly unlikely that God caused some evil calamity to come along just to hear you say thanks for it. In most cases it would be preferable to have avoided those horrible incidences in the first place.

God does not want rejoicing *for* bad things but rather *during* them. But even this is difficult. There are times when things seem so bad and dark that one might be tempted to say, "What's the use? My whole life just got flushed!"

It is not the teaching of Scripture to give thanks for all the junk that may hit us in life. It is the teaching of Scripture to find something to give thanks for—something of merit or value—while we are being hit by the junk.

Sometimes the things that have real value are subtle and often taken for granted. Sometimes they are things that do not suggest themselves until you compare your life with that of another who is even less fortunate. The truth of this verse is that Christians have something to thank God for even during the worst of times.

Think about one thing you could write a thank you note to God about right now.

Week Eleven

DWELL ON THESE THINGS

Day 1 Looking for the Good

> *Finally, brothers, whatever is true, whatever is*
> *noble, whatever is right, whatever is pure, whatever*
> *is lovely, whatever is admirable—if anything is*
> *excellent or praiseworthy—think about such*
> *things. Whatever you have learned or received or*
> *heard from me, or seen in me—put it into practice.*
> *And the God of peace will be with you.* Philippians
> 4:8,9

For some people the glass is half full, for others it is half
empty. For some the best is around the corner, for others the
worst is yet to come. Some people see the character of a person as pushy, others see it as outgoing.

With most things in life, and especially in people, things
can always be better. People can do their jobs a little bit better,
they can be a little more thoughtful or considerate of others.
They could be a little less grumpy in the morning or a show a
little more excitement at something nice done for them.

It is a rule that if you look hard enough for a flaw in things
or people you will surely find it. If you want to pick on somebody for something you probably won't have to look very long
to find it.

Now it is true that there are some things in which it is very
hard to find good. In fact, there are some people who are so
crabby and bitter that they have squeezed out of their life all of
the things that really are pleasant. There are some people
whose evil actions are so sinister that they override any good
thing that might surface in their lives. For example, Hitler may
have been kind to animals, a nice thing. But he was rotten to
people, which cancels out his kindness to animals.

But in most situations, with most things, and certainly
with most people, the negative things that are present do not
make that person or thing completely undesirable.

God's advice to us is to think on the good or positive side
of things and people. He does not want us to be ostrich-like
and fail to see the imperfect or even bad side of people. His

advice is often to disassociate with those of heavily polluted character (especially those who claim to be Christians). At the same time we are warned not to go around inspecting for the flaws and slivers in the eyes of others. The danger is that we will neglect our own sight maintenance program and be blinded by our own two-by-four.

Instead we are to look for the worth and value in something and someone. We are to think about the things that point up, not the things that point down. We are to be realists with a bent towards optimism, at least in the things that God is concerned with.

The next time that a situation comes up where criticism—deserved or undeserved—is ripe for the picking, try reaching out for some thought that will give the full picture, the kind picture, and possibly the true picture. Who knows—it just might come back to bless you someday!

Quietly examine your attitude about things and people. Do you have the tendency to be highly critical and picky? Ask God to help change the way that you see things.

Day 2 Annie: A True Story

> *May the Lord make your love increase and over-flow for each other and for everyone else, just as ours does for you.* 1 Thessalonians 3:12

"Tonight we are going to play a game," said the youth pastor. "This is a departure from what we normally do in our mid-week meeting but I hope that you will find some value in this experiment."

There were 12 people present in the little church hall that evening. It wasn't the entire youth group but it was the majority. Bill sat hunched over, his long arms and legs seemingly having trouble finding a place to fit. Marianne sat next to him, clean, well-groomed, and with an obvious taste for putting together clothing outfits. She was one of the cheerleaders at the local high school and was way up there on the popularity ladder. Phillip sat across from her, his glasses always slightly askew on his head and thousands of bits of information streaming through the computer that he called a brain. In the back row of chairs, two or three seats removed from the rest of the group, sat Annie. Chubby—no, overweight—poor complexion and eyesight, and void of much of the social grace that seemed to be so abundant with the rest of the group.

"We are going to play a game called Lifeboat," said the young minister. "I want you to imagine that you are 12 people in a lifeboat that can only hold 11. You have no idea how long that you might be at sea, or even if you will be rescued at all. You have a limited amount of food and water and the seas look as if they are going to rise, risking the chance of capsizing an overloaded boat. What will you do?"

It was one of those sticky situation-type games that are designed to make everyone wrestle with priorities and such. The players tonight quickly came to the agreement that one of the party would have to jump. But who?

The group went from person to person, evaluating the pluses and minuses for keeping them on board or offering them up. Bill was deemed too valuable to sacrifice because of his worth as a potential pro basketball player. Besides, they could use him as a mast if they fashioned a sail, someone joked. Marianne was also a sure bet to stay. Her beauty and charm made all the boys in the group reluctant to sacrifice this Venus to Neptune.

Even when the group came to Phillip the consensus was clear: this kid is going to be a brain surgeon or something. Besides, he is the only one who knows anything about astronomy and navigation.

But when the group got to Annie, there were no great declarations of her value or potential—only hemmed and hawed statements like, "Well, uh, Annie, uh, you shouldn't jump either, uh, you're a nice person." The truth was that even though Annie had been coming to the group for quite a few months no one had taken the time to get to know her or to think about what was good and valuable in her.

The game rotated around the group another time. The youth director gave them the three-minute warning to come up with a solution. The trend was going towards trying to risk it with all hands still on board when Annie said, "I'll jump." The youth worker summed up the evening with a brief talk, the message of which was lost on Annie. She was thinking about another message she had received.

That next day Annie did jump. She apparently could not think of a reason why not to, and neither could her "brothers and sisters" at the church.

If you were in the group, would you feel responsible for Annie's suicide? Why or why not? Are there any "Annies" in whom you need to find some worth?

Day 3 The Big Compliment

> *When Jesus saw Nathanael approaching, he said of him, "Here is a true Israelite, in whom there is nothing false."* John 1:47

Jesus did and said some very curious things. He used spit and dirt to make mud to cause a blind man to see. He caused demons to enter a herd of pigs, which then promptly ran themselves off a cliff (at no small financial loss to their owner). He told things in stories that were so cloaked in mystery that even his closest followers could not figure them out. And he said things about people. He referred to Peter, one of His best friends, as Satan. He called a foreign woman a "dog," which, in that culture, was a pretty rough thing to say. Then He turned around and said that a foreign soldier of the hated occupation force had more faith than anyone in Israel (which is kind of like telling a Nazi SS commander in occupied Paris that he is more spiritual than all of the Frenchmen).

He said something curious when He first saw Nathanael, who was to be one of His disciples. In general terms, He said, "Here is a guy who has a pure heart; he is not a manipulator or a bitter man. He is without deceit."

What a compliment! It shocked even Nathanael. "How do you know me?" he asked. If he had known Jesus he would never have asked that question. God is able to lift all the lids of our souls' hiding places. It is no use to say, just because we can't see Him, why bother to try? Nathanael had figured that one out, and since there was nothing but pure intentions in him towards God it could not help but tint his actions, thoughts, and behavior towards others.

Hidden motives, game playing, secret agendas tend to run contrary to the way of Christ.

Creating a decoy to fool or deceive our parents is a favorite pastime of many kids. Make them think that we are doing what we are actually not. Using a smoke screen to cover up our own failures and mistakes with others is another common ploy. Some go so far as to find a scapegoat to lay the blame on.

It is probably not necessary to describe the workings of deceit in detail. Most of us are very familiar with deceit. It is webbed throughout much of our lives. It tangles and twists its way into things that we wish it would stay away from. We call it "white lies," "harmless fibs," or "tall tales," but it is still deceit. We claim a technical victory—"I didn't actually lie." Instead, we deceived. Guile, deceit, plotting, bitterness—it is all the product of a mind set on something other than the best, the pure, the good.

If we have not reached the point where our lives are free from the stain of deceit and guile perhaps we can be motivated to clean up our lives by the desire to have Jesus say to all those around when we meet Him, "There is a person without deceit or guile."

What was the last deceitful thing that you did? Take some time and confess it to God.

Day 4 A Good Washing

> *There are those . . . who are pure in their own eyes*
> *and yet are not cleansed of their filth.* Proverbs
> 30:11,12

"I can read that; it doesn't affect me at all."

"Hey, I've seen worse stuff than that and I'm not some sort of kook!"

"What's wrong with listening to that? It doesn't bother me at all."

"If you think that is rude you ought to hear what all the other people say!"

Sound familiar? Sometimes the statements above are absolutely true. Sometimes they are a way of saying "Don't butt into my private life." Sometimes they are a way of saying "It may not look like it but I'm still clean."

We live in a dirty world. It is no more possible to live, work, and play on this globe and stay unaffected and uncontaminated spiritually than it is to wear the same white clothes every day and not get them soiled and stained. The pollutants are everywhere. They are in the books and magazines we read. They are in the music we listen to, the programs we see on TV, and the movies we watch. They call out to us from the newspaper stands and rub against us in the grocery store checkout line. They roll off the lips of friends, teachers, and even parents.

What makes for spiritual filth? Simply stated, it is anything that runs contrary to the ideas and Spirit of God. It is the kind of thinking and action that leads to the dismantling of a person's soul rather than the rebuilding of it. It is mold and decay on the new creature that we are supposed to be becoming.

Sometimes we pick the dirt up intentionally. Sometimes we stumble and fall into a puddle of cesspool thinking. Usually we just brush up against it and walk away wearing its mark. The important thing is that we realize our contamination and clean up the mess.

For Christians, to make the kind of statements that suggest the things in this world have no effect on them are self-deceiving. We are usually far more polluted than we think, and far more filthy than we can imagine. We collect the residue of a dirty world hour by hour and day by day. To suggest that we are pure when we are really reeking in decay is not only blindness but foolishness.

The best thing to do is to admit we need a good cleaning. We need it daily, often hourly. We need to redirect the thought desires and aspirations constantly. Staying pure takes a constant scrubbing by the Spirit of God. Anyone can be a filthy pig with no effort at all.

In what areas do you tend to get spiritually polluted quickly? Write a note to God asking for His cleansing in this area.

Day 5 Kick 'em When They're Down

> *Love does not delight in evil but rejoices with the truth.* 1 Corinthians 13:6

Why is it that we love a good rumor so much? Why is it that bad news spreads like it was carried on the wind and good news moves at a slug's speed? What is it in us that likes to kick 'em when they are down? What is it that finds joy or enjoyment in sordid details instead of finding sorrow or outrage?

I'm afraid it is something dark and sinister—a stripe of evil that ribbons across the human race. We are voyeurs of injustice even while we root for truth to win.

Perhaps we love to see someone fall because we can compare their failure to our success, rather than take warning that we are cut from the very same cloth as the fallen one.

Possibly we have so little of value to talk about or discuss that we find ourselves talking about people and their deeds so frequently. We are to be pitied for our shallowness as well as rebuked for our gossip.

Possibly because we have not yet come to grips with the idea that what gives God pleasure is what is to give us pleasure. His pure love is always looking for the justice. The truth. The good rather than the bad. When He sees the sin, He weeps; He does not rejoice.

Whatever the reason, it is quite clear that we often fill our time and conversation with the latest and the worst about so and so. In fact, some church "prayer chains" are more of an abomination than they are a ministry because of the fine line between getting the story right and gossip.

An interesting experiment would be to create a group of people who were committed to "good gossip"—talking about the good things that people have done or are doing—the nice things about their personality rather than the nasty things. Imagine what the response would be to people who visited this group during an average lunch at school. They would be amazed that there was this kind of love and care available in the world. They would certainly not be afraid of what might be said behind their backs. The members could help police each other so that nothing unkind was said. It would be revolutionary! It would also be very difficult.

This idea of siding with truth goes a lot further than just our conversation. It spills over into any area where someone is getting the raw end of the stick. It may mean going against what is popular at times. It makes us an activist in life. It makes us takes sides and try to pick up the person who is down.

Can you think of a recent time that you stood up for someone who was being belittled? Look for opportunities to side with truth today.

Day 6 A Clearing in the Fog

> *I will meditate on all your works and consider all your mighty deeds.* Psalm 77:12

Try to think about thinking. You cannot do it. You can

think about the objects that pop into your mind. You may be able to see yourself with a contemplative look on your face. But you cannot think about the process of thinking itself. Yet we all know that we do think, at least sometimes.

All thinking has something as its focus. Those things are gathered from our experience and exposure. They are the raw materials which we use to put together our ideas, perceptions, and ultimately our actions. If we use the wrong raw materials we will not end up with what we had hoped for in the end.

For instance, a person wishing to build a house could conceivably make it from a great number of materials—from tanned animal skins to tumbleweeds. The house may be adequate for much of the time but it may have tremendous problems during the first rainfall. We use the materials that we do to build a house because they prove durable enough to withstand most of what nature dishes out.

Much of the raw material that you have started to build your life with has already been handed out. Some of us have some pretty good stuff to work with, some of us have a load of junk. All of us could use some better materials and some decent blueprints. This is exactly what God wants to provide. He wants to change the inside of His people so that they have better raw material to work with and He wants to give them a blueprint of what to do with that raw material.

One of the primary ways that God began to change the composition of the bad quality materials in our lives is to become a focus in our thinking. When we think about Him or His ideas it changes the way we perceive and feel.

Many of the things on which we focus in the process of daily living do not contribute much to the restructuring of the raw materials in our lives. Much of it is simply fog.

The psalmist suggests that we meditate or focus in on God and His works. He gives a practical suggestion for clearing a spot in our mind where God can begin to do His work. He is asking us to have a way of thinking that pulls God into the picture all of the time.

Since our thinking is constructed of what we focus on, it makes sense to zero in on the One who is solid, sure, and eternal under any situation. To do otherwise is to build the house of our life with fog.

Make it a point to put God in all of your thoughts today. See what a difference it makes.

Week Twelve

BE CONTENT

Day 1 Few of Us

I rejoice greatly in the Lord that at last you have renewed your concern for me. Indeed, you have been concerned, but you had no opportunity to show it. I am not saying this because I am in need, for I have learned to be content whatever the circumstances. I know what it is to be in need, and I know what is is to have plenty. I have learned the secret of being content in any and every situation, whether well fed or hungry, whether living in plenty or in want. I can do everything through him who gives me strength. Philippians 4:10-13

Few of us are millionaires. Some of us were born to a fatherless family. Some of us were raised in broken homes. A few of us have had a succession of stepparents. Only a few of us have show-stopping beauty. A handful of us have suffered abuse and neglect from those we love. Good grades come hard to many of us as do athletics or pliable talents. Some of us have suffered the loss of a loved one. Some of us have been betrayed by friends.

For only a few of us the conditions of life have been smooth. Most of the rest of us have hit the chuckholes and ditches of crises. For some whose way is still smooth there are some big potholes waiting around the bend.

Many of the conditions are completely out of our control. Some could be improved with a little effort on our part. Sometimes we find ourselves in conditions forced on us by other people.

Some of us may suffer cruelly in the future. Others will get off with relative ease. Some of us may have a roller coaster life that swings from one high point to a desperate low.

Some of us will respond to what life shells out with anger, bitterness or rage. Others may try to cloud out the disappointment with a blur of chemicals. Some will hide behind a wall of fat, others will try to keep on the run. Some will sink into a bog of depression and aimlessness. Still others will plop themselves in front of a glowing TV screen and live out their lives vicariously through others. Some will simply choose to ignore the pain as if not dealing with it will make it better.

In the swirl of good and bad circumstances there are some who are content. They are not complacent; they recognize wrongs, pain, raw deals, but their life is built on another plane. They are a small band of people who not only talk and theorize about life on another dimension but actually live it. They are people whose peace and meaning in life is not derived from another person or from the state of their health or economy but from a desire to be like their Master. They are people who are undefeatable in this world simply because they are no longer of it.

On a scale of 1-10 (10 being content) how would you rate yourself?

Day 2 The Greedy Kid

Better one handful with tranquillity than two handfuls with toil and chasing after the wind. Ecclesiastes 4:6

Every spring the sunny little park across the street from my house was the sight for the kiddie Easter egg hunt. Early on Saturday morning members of a local civic group would arrive and begin hiding hundreds of small plastic eggs (redeemable for a prize) and foil-covered candy bunnies and eggs.

The park was sectioned off into divisions so that the preschoolers would not have to compete for goodies with the fourth graders and be trampled to death in the process. The officials had roped off the area and had posted guards to prevent premature pilfering of the prizes.

Living across the street from all the excitement, it was impossible to avoid being dragged over at the earliest possible time by my own two little boys who wanted to scout out the location of the golden egg in advance.

Soon all of the kids and parents arrived. Many of the little girls had on crisp, pastel Easter dresses that by the day's end would have a brown swath of chocolate running through them. The boys would all wear their melted candy from ear to ear like a five o'clock shadow.

The countdown began and the kids cranked up their greed impulses to a fever pitch. AHOOGAH! went the air horn and the little treasure-seekers piled onto the velvety grass, and onto each other, in a frantic attempt to collect as many bits of candy and eggs as possible and bring them back to their parents waiting behind the line with Easter baskets or paper bags.

One little ankle-biter had seemingly figured out that multiple trips to home base would not be the way to go. He decided to load his chubby little arms with as many goodies as he could carry. I watched in fascination as he methodically bent down and picked up egg after egg and cradled each piece precariously against his small chest. He made some distance into the fertile field of candy when he decided that it was time to go back with his booty.

About this time another kid accidentally swung around and bumped the little fellow. His full arms sent a shower of candy all around. The other children began to scoop up the stray candy and soon the sight resembled pint-sized little sharks in a feeding frenzy.

The original owner of the candy collected as much as he could and waddled towards his mother on the sidelines. As he stumbled along the lawn, bits of his treasure dribbled off of his pile to be swept up by the other children who had by now turned into full-fledged vultures. By the time the kid got back to home base with his fumbled pile the hunt was over.

His collection was so paltry and lonely at the bottom of his Easter basket that other parents around dumped their children's excess into his collection.

In his primitive little greed he had come back almost empty-handed. But then greed is like that for all of us. The more we try to carry, the less that we really end up with.

Create a motto which will help remind you of the foolishness of greed.

Day 3 I Can Do All Things

I can do everything through him who gives me strength. Philippians 4:13

Once there was a little boy who found a rock protruding a few inches under the surface of his sand box. With his little plastic tools he dug around the rock. It was quite a large rock in comparison to the little boy. Still, he scraped and dug furiously, eventually trenching completely around the intruder to his little world.

Although he was now able to tilt the rock back and forth he could not seem to grasp it with enough strength to pull it out of the hole. Finally, with great frustration he was able to use his legs and hands to roll the stone out of its hole and into the flat sand of the sandbox.

The next obstacle was to get the rock to the edge of the sandbox and over the side. The rock rolled well enough to the edge of the box but the final hurdle proved too much for the strength of the little child.

After pinched fingers and numerous vain attempts the little child burst into tears of despair. A moment later he noticed the shadow of his father falling over the little sandbox. "I have been watching you try to move that rock for a long time, Son," said the father gently. "But Son, you should have used all the strength that you had."

At this the boy was exasperated. "I did," he whined.

"No, Son." replied his father as he lifted the rock out of the sandbox with great ease. "You did not use all of your strength. You did not ask *me*."

The pathway to contented living is full of a great many rocks and boulders around which there seems to be no way. To move them seems an insurmountable task, and it will be, unless we use all of the strength available to us.

Living in a society that cannot curb its appetite for material things, where even relationships are disposed of rather than be repaired if they break, we cannot help but be smudged and stained by the ideas and values that cause us to become restless with what God has given to us. We can leave these rocks and stones in the sandbox of our lives or we can use all of our strength to yank them out or break them into sand.

Take some time and ask God for His strength in something you are facing today.

Day 4 Many Have None

But godliness with contentment is great gain. For we brought nothing into the world, and we can take nothing out of it. But if we have food and clothing, we will be content with that. 1 Timothy 6:6-8

I am fascinated by people who can achieve things that I cannot. I am fascinated by people who can climb up the vertical face of a cliff with no gear and only their strength to keep them in place. I'm fascinated by people who can remember numbers by only seeing them once. It took me fifteen years to remember my driver's license number and I still forget my Social Security number.

I'm fascinated by people who can do effortlessly what is extremely complex and difficult for me. I'm fascinated the most by people who can take a very tough idea and live by it.

One day I noticed that a friend of mine always wore the same shoes. Now this probably would not have struck me odd if it were a man, because many guys will wear a pair of shoes for every occasion until they are too ratty to lace and then they'll go buy a new pair. What struck me odd is that this friend is a woman.

At first I did not know if I should comment on my observation. After all it was really none of my business if she wanted to wear the same pairs of shoes all of her life. Maybe she had a dozen pair of shoes that were all the same style and color—some sort of shoe fetish. But that was not the case. In fact, each time I saw her I would instinctively look to see if she had the same pair of "old faithfuls" on. (The shoes were not odd or unattractive but rather non-descript and neutral.)

Most of the women that I know and a great many men as well have a closet full of shoes from which to select. Apparently this friend did not.

Because in friendships you can get away asking things that might be too rude to ask a casual acquaintance I decided to get an explanation from her. "Say, can I ask you a question about your shoes?" I asked one day.

She looked up at me and smiled and said "Sure."

"Well, I was just wondering, do you ever wear any other shoes?"

She was quiet for just a moment and then replied, "No, I don't have any other shoes."

I shifted uneasily in my seat. I knew that she was a single mother of two boys and did not have a ton of spare change to line a wardrobe with. She could sense that I was not about to venture any further onto the ice so she continued. "You see, I can only afford to buy the boys one pair of shoes, and it does not seem fair for me to have more than what I can get them. Besides, I feel lucky to have one pair of shoes; there are many people who do not have any."

That night I went home fascinated again. I sat on the edge of my bed and looked into my closet full of shoes and prayed that I could get to the place where I could be content with just food and covering—and one pair of shoes.

Could you be content with only one pair of shoes? Why or why not?

Day 5 No Competition

Since we live by the Spirit, let us keep in step with the Spirit. Let us not become conceited, provoking and envying each other. Galatians 5:25,26

There is a game that many people, young and old, play called "Keeping Up with the Joneses." The simple strategy of this game is to make sure that your friend or neighbor does not outdo you in the acquisition of material goods, influence, or power. It is a game that nobody claims to play but many actually do. Some of its biggest detractors are its most ardent supporters—in secret, of course.

Sometimes the game is played with only one other person, often times without his or her knowledge. He or she becomes the target, the one to beat, the enemy. What triggers the game in the heart of the competitor varies from individual to individual. Sometimes it is raw jealousy of the skill, talent, popularity or natural beauty of another person. Sometimes it is the need to stand a little taller in the eyes of those around us, even if it means standing on the reputation of our competition.

In most cases competition tends to bring out the worst in us. Whether it is for one-upmanship with the person next door or in a group setting over a football team that we happen to owe allegiance to, competition wants to see the other fall— and to glory in it.

Competition appeals to our pride, which is the most deadly sin of all. Competition demands the spotlight, craves the attention and begs for applause.

Competition is not the ways of those who want the best for the other person. It is not consistent with those directives that come from the Spirit of God living inside of us.

Keeping up with the Joneses has no other point than to say, "I'm the better one." It heavily contrasts the ideas of humility and kindness that lead those following Christ to say,

"I count all my personal achievements as rubbish, that I might gain Christ."

Competition always has a loser, someone who walks away with hung head or angry spirit. In fact, competition has two losers because the winner often loses sight of his or her own finiteness and steps into the chair of self-deification. A place where he or she does not belong. Competition means that there will be a new kid in town will do it a little better, faster or with more skill to grab the spotlight for a little while. Leaving the loser to talk about what used to be.

It is no wonder we are urged to avoid competing with each other. The game is rigged. We have lost it the minute we begin to play.

Can you think of a person that you envy or find yourself trying to beat? Ask God to help you change your attitude towards that person.

Day 6 Your Heart's Desire

> *Delight yourself in the Lord and he will give you*
> *the desires of your heart.* Psalm 37:4

As a child I was intrigued by the various fairy tales which involved wishes—Aladdin's Lamp, The Monkey Paw, and other stories in which some character got the chance at three or so wishes. Of course as you remember, the people in the stories always blew it by wishing for some terrible thing and then using up their wishes to get rid of the mess they made.

I always thought that the characters lacked imagination. If they had thought about it for any bit of time they would have simply wished for a dozen more wishes to come true, and kept multiplying their heart's desire.

With a quiver of wishes guaranteed I could certainly think of quite a shopping list that I would like to see appear before my very eyes. Naturally they were the wishes of a child so they had much more to do with toys, pets and tricky devices than they had with things that grownups might have wished for.

I'm afraid that if I had gotten my heart's desire at that stage in life it would have made me one spoiled child and would have been quite useless in a few years time.

God comes incredibly close to the promises of those old fairy tales by offering to give us the desires of our heart. What does He mean? Is this an invitation to scoop up all the goodies that life has to offer? To claim the promise for a new sports car?

God is very serious about keeping His word; could it mean that He really does want us to yearn and seek after the things that we want and that He will give them to us? Hardly.

The condition of the promise is that we delight ourselves in the Lord. He is what we want. He is what we enjoy. He is what we desire. If this is the case, then He will give Himself to us.

It is difficult if not impossible to delight ourselves with God if we have our head clouded with other desires. We cannot want two things with the same intensity. We cannot serve two masters.

Christians are supposed to be unique in the sense that they have changed desires; they have given up wishes. They long to just delight themselves in God. Period. Please avoid thinking that this sounds too simplistic. Delighting in God is not simple at all, for He is not simple. It is a longing towards the complex and demanding, not a bask in the sun.

It is this one goal that helps bring the contentment that all those who truly follow Christ experience. That growling desire, that long unfulfilled emptiness, has finally been filled by changing what it is that delights us. When we trade in all those things that don't really matter for the only One who really does, suddenly contentment floods our soul. Suddenly our wishes are fulfilled.

Memorize this Psalm 37:4 and repeat it to yourself every day this coming week.